WAR OF & Weddings

A Legacy of Two Fathers
BY JERRY YELLIN

Sunstar
PUBLISHING LTD.

OF WAR AND WEDDINGS
A LEGACY OF TWO FATHERS
by Jerry Yellin
©
United States Copyright, 1995
Sunstar Publishing, Ltd.
116 North Court Street
Fairfield, Iowa 52556

First Edition 1995
Printed in the United States of America

Library of Congress Catalog Card Number: 94 - 069 - 576

ISBN 0 - 9638502 - 5 - 3

Cover Design: David Bordow
Editing: Elizabeth Pasco and Rodney Charles

What we leave behind, the sum total of our experiences, is our legacy. This is the story of two men influenced by conflict, who, through their children, have found peace and love.

To my wife Helene, my sons and their families.
To Taro and Hatsue and my family in Japan,
may they live in a world of peace and harmony
for all of their days and more.

Contents

Acknowledgments vii

Chapter One   *The Journey* 3

Chapter Two   *Sen* 11

Chapter Three   *The War* 23

Chapter Four   *Discovering Japan* 39

Chapter Five   *Kenrokuen* 49

Chapter Six   *Robert's Trip* 57

Chapter Seven   *Meeting Takako* 65

Chapter Eight   *Dilemma* 81

Chapter Nine   *Reflections* 95

Chapter Ten   *The 78th Fighter Squadron* 115

Chapter Eleven   *Losing Friends* 137

Chapter Twelve   *Home from War* 153

Chapter Thirteen   *Yas* 179

Chapter Fourteen   *The Bomb* 195

Chapter Fifteen   *Robert's Meeting* 213

Chapter Sixteen   *The Wedding* 227

Chapter Seventeen   *The Fathers* 251

Afterword 275

Contents

Acknowledgments

This book began as a magazine article written in the spring of 1988, superbly edited by Kevin Brass, a friend of my son, Robert. It was published in the December issue of *San Diego Magazine*. The article was voted best feature article in publications with circulations of 100,000 or more by the San Diego Press Club.

Friends asked me to expand the article into a book. Raymond Buckland and then Jack Forem, both published authors and friends of mine, were instrumental in getting me started. Jack Lambert, historian, generously allowed me to corroborate my memories and to use material from his book, *The Pineapple Air Force*.

When I moved to Fairfield, Iowa in 1991 and needed space to write, Cooper Norman and Jonathan Lipman volunteered an office. They provided computers, printers, faxes, phones and friendship in abundance. Rodney Charles of Sunstar Publishing read my manuscript and made the decision to publish the book. All that I needed was an editor. Sunstar provided her as well. When I met Elizabeth Pasco and she agreed to work with me, I was elated. She has inspired me and gently persuaded me to greater heights.

Bill and Lillian Darr, my dear friends, have read draft after draft adding insight and help that has encouraged me when I needed it most.

Of course, without Robert and Takako there is no story, no book.

The two who are closest to me, providing tender

care and attention throughout this seven-year process are my second son, Steven, and Helene, my loving wife. I am sure that any of my four sons would have done the same, but Steven has always been nearby. Sometimes as close as the next room, always within walking distance. When ego and possession loomed, he was the one who put me back on course. If this story has universal appeal it is because of Steven's gentle wisdom and great love for his father.

As I write this, Helene and I are nearing our 45th wedding anniversary. Through the years she has led me from the darkness of war to the bright light that has always surrounded her. Her innocence and purity astound me. She is a literary person and loves books. Her encouragement, her intelligence and knowledge, and enthusiasm have helped me overcome any doubts about my ability to write.

To all of you I give my heartfelt thanks.

CHAPTER ONE

The Journey

I SAW JAPAN for the first time from the cockpit of a P-51 on April 7, 1945. We were the first land-based fighter planes to fly a mission against the Japanese Empire. At the morning briefing before take off, the intelligence officer told us, "When you fly across Suruga Bay, focus your gun cameras on the tip of Mount Fuji. In that way we will be able to evaluate your film when you fire your guns at the enemy." We needed a centering point for the rings of our gun sight, to see if our guns were firing where they were aimed. The mountain loomed skyward to 12,000 feet, its snow-covered peak glistened in the morning sun, a picture indelibly imprinted on my mind.

In October 1982 my wife, Helene, and I boarded a Singapore Airline 747 at Los Angeles International Airport for a flight to Tokyo. It had been thirty-seven years since I had flown the last mission against my World War II enemy. I had received an invitation to go to Japan for three weeks on a business trip as part of a lecture team. It was the first time that I had thought about Japan as a place to visit. I hadn't dwelt on the war, or even thought much about it, until then.

It was over, and I had lived my life without looking back. Never had I spoken of my war experiences. Occasionally I mentioned flying, or bailing out off the coast of Hawaii to my children. But I had never gone into any detail about my life as a combat pilot, not even to Helene. As I settled back in the comfortable business-class seat, my mind drifted back in time.

On my eighteenth birthday, February 15, 1942, I had enlisted in the Army Air Corps. The application required my parents' signatures before I could take the examination for Aviation Cadet. They held back as long as they could. They were not eager for me to go off to war and thought I should wait to be drafted.

Reluctantly, my parents signed the necessary papers. I passed the mental exam but failed the physical when it was discovered that I had only 20/30 vision in the left eye. The doctor said I could take the test again in a week and would be accepted into the program if I passed then. I remained in a darkened room and ate carrots for three days prior to the examination. As luck would have it, my mother was on the draft board and she brought me the eye chart to memorize! I passed the test the second time and in August 1942 I reported for induction into the Army Air Corps as an Aviation Cadet.

My obsession was to fly a fighter plane against the Japanese. . . .

Images of war were engraved in the minds of all of us who had been in combat. They surfaced from time to time, day or night, triggered by events, something we heard or they just crept into our minds at odd times. It happened to me once in a movie theater. Helene and I had flown to San Francisco to celebrate our son Michael's 30th birthday. Michael was a resident physician at Pacific Presbyterian Medical Center. The day after the party was miserable and cold, so we all decided to see a film. The movie *Platoon* had just opened and had received good reviews. Helene suggested that we see it. Michael, his wife Gail, David, our oldest son, Helene and I went to the film together. I was not prepared for what I saw on the screen nor for what happened to me.

The movie was a devastating story of ground soldiers in Vietnam, their fight to survive the war and their inner, tormented battles to maintain some sense of humanity. I drifted off from time to time, inward to my memory, a memory of war that I had carried for forty-one years. As the screen showed bodies being thrown into a large pit, a bulldozer moving dirt and dead bodies into a mass grave, I started to cry uncontrollably.

When the film ended I couldn't get out of my seat. I sat there and sobbed for fifteen minutes. Helene looked alarmed and kept stroking my head. When I calmed down, Michael asked, "What happened Dad? Are you all right?"

"I'll be all right in a minute. It's just . . . the screen showed pictures that have been in my mind all these years . . . Japanese soldiers, mounds of them, slowly being pushed into mass graves on Iwo Jima."

As soon as I was able, we left the theater and walked the rainy streets of San Francisco for an hour. Helene never let go of my hand. That night I spoke to her about the war for the first time.

In the spring of 1945, I flew my P-51 from Saipan to Iwo Jima to join the war against the Japanese. The Marines had landed on Iwo in February and secured a dirt runway at the foot of Mount Suribachi, memorialized by the famous photograph of Marines raising the flag on its summit. I was a member of the 78th Fighter Squadron assigned to the 7th Fighter Wing, under the command of Brigadier General Mickey Moore. I landed on that dirt runway.

We dive-bombed and strafed the Japanese defenders who were dug deeply into caves in the hillsides of the island. The Marine mortuary was alongside our squadron base and every day we saw truckloads of U.S. Marines, killed in battle, being brought in and laid out for identification and burial. Everywhere we looked there were hills of bulldozed Japanese bodies, and the smell of death filled the air. Later, mass graves were dug and the bodies were pushed into the ground and covered.

We lived in foxholes dug into the sand and rock of the island. On the ground, we fought to survive terrifying Banzai raids, which were suicide attacks by *sake*-drunk Japanese defenders who thought it an honor to die, so long as they took as many enemy soldiers as possible with them. From the air, we dropped napalm into cave openings, driving the Japanese soldiers out to waiting Marine rifle and mortar fire.

We went to the front, looking for souvenirs in the same caves we had dive-bombed and strafed. There we saw the results of flame-throwers, "freezing" soldiers into hideous positions. And we attended memorial services for our fellow pilots, for whom the war had ended. What I saw on Iwo has remained with me ever since.

Now, as the 747 approached Japan after the long flight over the Pacific from California, I asked the steward to see if he could get me into the cockpit. This is forbidden on domestic airlines but permissible on some foreign carriers at the discretion of the captain.

"Please tell him an old World War II fighter pilot wants to see Japan again from a pilot's perspective, to view Mount Fuji as he saw it on his first day in combat."

A few minutes later the steward returned with a message:

"The captain asks that you come up to the flight deck whenever you desire, Mr. Yellin. He will be delighted to have you."

I left my seat immediately and entered the huge cockpit of this giant airliner. After introducing me to the co-pilot and the engineer, the captain extended an invitation to stay for the landing. I gladly accepted. Then, as I sat down on the jump seat behind the pilot, I looked out of the cockpit window in the direction of Fuji. I caught sight of the famous peak but my mind froze on another image—I saw again the faces of my dead comrades, the piles of Marine bodies waiting identification, the bloated, maggot-filled bodies of the Japanese soldiers. The smell of death filled my nostrils once more.

Overcome with emotion, I had to leave the cockpit and compose myself, before we landed in Tokyo.

The first few days in Japan were extremely difficult. I did not tell Helene, though she must have suspected. As we walked through the streets of Tokyo, I would catch her looking at me as I stared up at the sky. I saw the lights of a thousand bombs exploding across the ground. I saw crippled, burning planes falling from the sky. I pictured the B-29s dropping their bombs on the city.

The sights were triggering more memories than I was prepared for. They came into my awareness as I looked into the faces of the people on the streets and, disturbingly, as I lay in bed at night. I needed some quieter space to let my mind recuperate from the sudden, unexpected onslaught.

CHAPTER TWO

Sen

IT HAS ALWAYS been easy for me to talk to strangers when we travel and, sometimes, to make friends. In England one year, we needed directions to a subway. When I asked my seat mate at a concert where the nearest entrance was, he not only described where it was but walked with us to make sure we found it. The next day he called our hotel and invited us for lunch. We became friends. I didn't expect that in Japan for several reasons, the least of which was the language barrier and my unresolved feelings about the war. I was wrong.

We met Sen Matsuda quite by accident on the bullet train (Shinkansen) that travels the Tokaido Line from Tokyo to Osaka. He was seated with his wife in the first car. I noticed him immediately as we scanned the car for an empty seat.

He looked like a Buddha. His smooth, brown skin was taut on the bones of his face, and he had large beautiful eyes. He was clearly an elderly man, quite gaunt, but without wrinkles. He was elegantly dressed in blue leather pants and a brown leather jacket. His eyes sparkled and shone.

He was looking my way as I placed the luggage on the rack over the seats. Our eyes met for an instant and I knew that I would have to speak with him before we reached our destination.

He too felt something pass between us in that short contact of our eyes. He told me that later as we talked.

Soon after we pulled out of the station, vendors moved through the cars selling hot tea and coffee. These were followed by girls selling box lunches. Most of our fellow travelers bought something, and soon they were busy eating. The boxes were made of wood and were wrapped and tied with string or ribbon. At each station, as passengers left, they placed their re-tied boxes neatly in a pile. The boxes were collected at several stops. Absolutely no litter was left by anyone.

The opportunity to meet Mr. Matsuda came when I had a problem purchasing a cup of tea from the vendor. Noticing my difficulty expressing my wishes to her in Japanese, he leaned across the aisle and softly whispered, in perfect English, "She doesn't sell tea, only coffee."

"*Arigato Gozimasu,*" I said, and he responded again in perfect English, "Don't mention it." With that, our friendship began.

Spontaneously, we both got up and, standing in the aisle of the rapidly moving train, introduced ourselves.

"Your face glows with energy and contentment," I said, "and I felt I had to speak with you."

We exchanged business cards and started talking

about the book he was holding.

"It's an Australian novel," he said. "I'm reviewing it for a friend." He paused. I had never heard of the book. "By the way," he asked, "have you read the book *Roots* by Alex Hailey?"

"Of course," I replied. "It is one of my favorites. I bought copies of it for several of my friends just after it was published."

He looked at me for a moment and said, "I translated it into Japanese." He did not say this to impress me (although it certainly did), but to convey the fact that he knew a lot about America.

The train was approaching our stop, and I was afraid that we would not see each other again. Just before we started to gather our luggage together, he asked if we would be able to visit him in Chigasaki City before we left Japan.

"Please come to our home for lunch," he said. "We can continue our talk then."

"We have a tight schedule. I'll have to call you. I hope we can arrange it."

We shook hands warmly, the train stopped, and from the platform, we waved good-bye to our new friend.

I wanted to spend some time with Sen Matsuda, our new friend from the train. I had our schedule rearranged to include lunch with Mr. Matsuda the day before our trip to Kyoto.

The ride to his home in Chigasaki City, a suburb of Tokyo, took an hour. As our train eased to a stop at the station, we saw him standing on the platform, peering into each car as it passed, looking for us. He was dressed in a beautiful, full-length kimono. As we stepped off the train, he walked slowly toward us, accompanied by a young lady.

His daughter, Midori, had arrived from Tokyo a few minutes earlier, summoned to help her mother with the lunch. Midori looked much like her father. She had a warm, friendly face and a personality to match. The four of us walked out of the station for the short taxi drive to their home.

When we arrived at the house, we were greeted by Mrs. Matsuda. She was smaller than Sen, about 5-foot-2, quite thin and slight, and spoke English well. She greeted us with warmth and gestured for us to follow. Much to our surprise, instead of the sparsely furnished Japanese decor that we had expected, we saw a room completely furnished in a Western mode. We sat on a large stuffed Victorian-style couch in front of a low antique coffee table. Mr. and Mrs. Matsuda each sat on high-backed stuffed chairs on either side. The floor was covered with a Persian carpet.

Mrs. Matsuda served us tea and sweets, according to the custom. My friend thanked us for coming. "I am honored," he said. "I did not think that I could make new friends, especially foreign ones, at my age. I am seventy-five now, and nearing the end of my life."

"Come now," I replied. "You look fit and have a healthy inner glow."

"Yes, that is true, but I have had surgery for cancer, and you know what that can mean. I am aware that I can pass on at any time, so I have been spending all of these precious days in beautiful places, and looking at beautiful things. I want to live the rest of my life seeing and hearing only the wonders that man has created. I want to remember only the beauty. I want to view again all of the natural wonders of my country, so that I can take them with me when I begin the next great journey."

Mrs. Matsuda and Midori prepared lunch in the kitchen while Helene and I sat talking to Sen, sipping a fine Bordeaux. When Mrs. Matsuda called us to the dining room, a huge pot that smelled delicious was steaming on the table.

"I must flavor our lunch," he said. "This is a recipe for *sukiyaki* that my father taught me, and it has to be just so. My wife doesn't trust her taste and wants me to finish flavoring the dish." We watched as he poured *sake* from a large bottle, then, smelling the steam, he added other ingredients.

When he was satisfied, we were asked to join the family for lunch. We ate on dishes using Western utensils.

Lunch was exquisite. We ate and talked for more than an hour. At times I felt I was with old, dear friends. But I also thought, "this man had been my enemy." He was the first Japanese man I had met who spoke English well enough and was of the age that he might have served in the military. I gathered my courage and asked him about his experiences in the war.

When he replied, he spoke slowly and carefully.

"I was a young man when my country began its preparation for war," he said. "I was born in 1914, the year that World War I started, and I spent my early years in Tokyo. When I was seventeen, Japan began its disastrous adventure by invading Manchuria. Our people were told that we needed to become completely self-sufficient: no dependency on the outside world for the raw materials necessary to sustain our needs. The oil and minerals in China would help Japan become a 'self-sufficient' nation.

"Of course, we were never told about the atrocities committed by our invading armies, or our brutal treatment of the Chinese people. All that we saw or heard were glowing stories of the conquest and the brightness of Japan's future.

"I only learned about our history when I went to the United States to study in 1938. Your newspapers and newsreel movies showed pictures that I could not, did not, want to believe. I clearly remember a photograph of a small baby crying in the streets while fires burned around her in the bombed city.

"I have never, ever forgotten that picture. It remained with me when I returned home to Japan in 1940.

"The plans to fight a war with the United States and the Soviet Union had already become apparent in 1936 when a change in our government gave power to supporters of our aggressive military command. Not satisfied with the success in China, they formulated a five-year plan, agreed to by the Diet, to build a 'fighting-machine' large enough to take on the United States and the Soviet Union. Our leaders felt that victories over these two countries would secure Japan's position as the dominant force in Asia.

"The plan was truly audacious. It called for the build-up of war materials from the country we would use them on, the United States. Japan's steel production would be tripled with the purchase of iron and oil from America. Factories would be built with machines from the United States and Germany. A stockpile of raw materials would be accumulated for sustaining an all-out war for two years, the time our leaders thought it would take to win.

"None of this was revealed to the public. I only became aware of the depth of planning after I graduated from college and joined the government as an economist.

"I was opposed to the war from the beginning. My father and I both attended school in America. Not only did we not believe what we were being told by our government, we knew the might of your country first hand. The newspapers were full of speeches by our military leaders. 'The Americans have no stomach for war,' they said. 'All they are interested in is having good times. When we start the war, they will last for two weeks, surrender, and then we can proceed to occupy the territories we want and need for our expanding economy.'

"We knew better but were desperately afraid to speak up. I worked for the government, and I know that my views were shared by many. I truly felt the Emperor could have prevented the war, but he did nothing except echo the words of the military leaders.

"Then came what our government called 'the glorious attack on Pearl Harbor'."

Matsuda San drifted off into silence and we sat for a long time caught up in our private memories.

Suddenly I heard Mr. Matsuda's voice again. I had

missed some of his words, but I forced myself to tune back in.

"I was determined to live through the war," he was saying. "I knew that we would be attacked in due time, and I prepared myself for that eventuality. We were all issued helmets and gas masks. Every day there were drills on what to do if Tokyo was attacked. I listened and learned well. I never left my helmet anywhere. It was with me wherever I went, and this was years before any serious aerial bombing began. My colleagues made jokes, sometimes to my face, but I did not care. I was not going to die in a war from lack of protection. If my time came, so be it, but I would not be left unprotected.

"When the B-29s finally came they were terrifying. The fire bombs would outline an area and then uncountable bombs were dropped inside the fires. The explosions were devastating. The fires ran unchecked throughout the city.

"One day my assistant left the office for home only to return in a complete daze. He could not find a trace of his house, and his entire family was missing. Wife, children, mother, father; all gone. He had no one to turn to, no place to live. For weeks he wandered through our office building as if in a dream. He slept in the office, ate in the office and finally came to accept his fate. All of us suffered losses. No one escaped some tragedy. And still I carried my helmet. It became my shield against danger, even after the 'all-clear' had sounded.

"Once the bombings started, Tokyo became the most dangerous place in the Empire, even more dangerous than the front. And still our leaders thought we would defeat America, but they had awakened a sleeping giant that would not rest until we were conquered.

"I remember one raid in particular. It was in April and began in midmorning. The bombers were escorted by American fighters for the first time. They came in much lower than before and we could see wave after wave filling the entire sky for hours. Again the fires started and then the winds began to blow. The fire spread from section to section and by evening were lighting the night sky like daylight. I lived many miles from the fires, but at eleven that night I could read a newspaper in the street in front of my house. That's how light it was. On that day 80,000 Japanese died and that was only the beginning."

CHAPTER THREE

The War

I WATCHED MR. MATSUDA intently as he calmly recounted his story. Tears slowly welled up in my eyes as I listened to his words.

I had flown on that first escorted raid.

I remember telling a war correspondent from the *New York Times* that I saw little dots of light spring from the ground as the bombs exploded. Wave after wave of bombers dropped their cargo inside the squares of fire on the ground. We fighter pilots were in a constant state of alert; Japanese fighters were all over the sky and the aerial battles between us were fierce. We had to protect our "Big Brothers"—the B-29s—as they droned on and on over the target. When I had a chance to look down, I could see fires raging. All of the city, it seemed, was on fire.

Triggered by Mr. Matsuda's words, memories started to come back in a flood.

His words recreated images in my mind that I had tried desperately to forget. At that moment the past was as real as the present—I had slipped back in time. It was shortly after we had set up base on Iwo Jima. We knew we had been shipped to Iwo to fly combat missions, but suddenly we had our first order.

The sixteen senior pilots in our squadron were to fly eight hundred miles over the waters of the Pacific to Japan, in single-engine fighter planes, to escort B-29s of the 73rd Bomber Wing as they attacked the Nakajima aircraft plant at Tokyo. We would protect the bombers from Japanese fighter planes until their work was done; then we would turn around and fly the eight hundred miles back to Iwo Jima.

This was to be the first "Very Long Range Fighter Escort" of B-29s over Japan. Only pilots with 800 to 1,000 hours of flying were chosen. There would be well over four hundred B-29s, and a total of one hundred fighter pilots flying P-51 Mustangs. Take-off was at 7:00 A.M. We were to be over the target from 10:45 A.M. till 11:30 A.M., and expected to return to Iwo again at 2:15 in the afternoon.

We took off and assembled in formation. Major John Piper of the 47th Squadron was the group leader. Gil Snipes led the 45th and Jim Vande Hey led the 78th—my squadron.

We rendezvoused with the B-29s at 18,000 feet over Kozu Shima, an island off the coast of the Izu Peninsula. Each fighter was carrying a heavy load, with two 110 gallon drop-tanks. As we crossed the coast of the mainland, we dropped the wing tanks and prepared to face enemy aircraft. The P-51s of the 78th Fighter Squadron were flying the right front quarter position, leading the whole formation and thus becoming the first land-based fighter squadron over mainland Japan.

Everything seemed to be going smoothly. We

had climbed to 30,000 feet to be "high cover," protecting the bombers from attack. It was from there that I watched the bombs explode like tiny firecrackers in the city. I could see pinpoints of light where the bombs hit, and then the sparks would come together to form a massive fire with thick black smoke that rose to 25,000 feet.

The fighting and the flak was intense. At one point I saw one of our B-29s get hit, and the right wing fell off. The plane burst into flames, and then, as if it was all being photographed in slow motion, one parachute came out, then a second, and a third; then the huge, lumbering plane just keeled over like a ship in the water, went into a spin, and fell from the sky. Of the twelve crew members on board, only three had bailed out.

We stayed over Japan for nearly an hour; then, when one of our pilots called in that he was running low on fuel, we turned for home. By 2:30 P.M., all of the aircraft had landed back at Iwo.

Despite seven hours and thirty-five minutes of exhausting over-water flying and nearly an hour of life-and-death combat with Japanese aircraft, every single fighter pilot got back safely. Of the bombers, only three were lost; two by anti-aircraft fire and only one, possibly, brought down by enemy aircraft. A total of eighty Japanese planes were destroyed.

Upon landing we found how dangerously low on fuel we were. I had only eight gallons left in my tank. What we didn't know then, was that we had run into what would later be called the "jet stream"—200 mph winds that we flew into head-on all the way back from

Japan. That's why we nearly ran out of gas.

Most of us had difficulty just getting out of our planes. We had been sitting in those tight cockpits for almost eight hours, flying without automatic pilots, navigating without navigation equipment. I was helped out of the plane by my crew chief. Hardly able to stand, we walked to a tent for the debriefing of that historic mission. Some one said his "butt was sprung," so that became the name for the condition; butt sprung.

A few weeks later a large Quonset hut was erected and equipped with bath tubs made of 100-gallon wing tanks that had been cut in half. Massage tables lined the entire side of the room. The tubs were filled with steaming hot, smelly, sulfur water just before we returned from a mission. From then on, we were debriefed then taken to the "Olde Iwo Jima Spa" for a hot bath, cold beer and a sandwich. *Iwo* means sulfur in Japanese. The water came out of the underground hot springs at 130°F. The Navy construction battalion, fondly known as the Seabees, tapped into the underground water supply, connected hoses and a pump, and the spa was born. Their reward was a substantial supply of hard liquor, courtesy of the flight surgeons office. After the hot bath and massage, our first priority was sleep. For me, that was hard to come by.

I remember telling the flight surgeon about the tremendous letdown after we began the flight home. I had watched my gas gauge go steadily down to empty, knowing I had to switch tanks or my engine would quit, yet not caring. Other pilots described similar experiences.

On the next and all subsequent missions, we were given benzedrine to take, one hour before we reached our target area. We'd fly two hours, take a pill, go on to the target, do our work, then fly four hours home. An hour after our interrogation, I would fall flat on my face with exhaustion as the drug wore off. All of us lost weight. I started the war weighing 160 pounds, but I weighed only 126 pounds at the end.

Our routine was to fly one long-range mission, followed by a local mission on Iwo and a short-range mission to knock out radar on nearby Chichi Jima. Then we would begin the rotation over by flying a long-range mission again, to the Japanese mainland. I flew each mission three times—once the night before, then the actual mission itself, and then again in vivid detail after I returned.

The evening before a mission, our names would be posted on the board. We knew we would be flying the next day, but we didn't know what the mission was, where the targets were, whether we would escort bombers or carry rockets—we just knew we had an assignment. For me, those nights were always sleepless, full of speculations and visions of possible destinations, with all their potential dangers.

We generally received information about the mission at a briefing before sunrise and then took off for Japan. As soon as we returned, practically as soon as we hit the runway, the questions began. Our crew chief would grab us first. He wanted to know if the airplane had performed properly. "Did everything work okay? Did you get in to the target?" Sometimes engines ran rough or guns wouldn't fire and the pilot would abort his mission, remaining with the escort B-29 off the coast of Japan. This was a concern for the crew chief, and they always asked how the engine performed. They took great pride in their work and did not like to let their pilot down.

Then while in the hot bath and with a cold beer, we were interrogated by the Intelligence Officers.

"What did you see?"

"What did you do?"

"Any kills?"

"What was the flak like?"

"How was the weather?"

"Were the maps accurate?"

We were in an agitated emotional state. They shot questions at us like reporters at a press conference and expected complete, detailed answers.

We answered as well as we could. The images in our minds at the time were extremely vivid, but we were so charged up that it was hard to talk.

After the debriefing, there was another round of questioning. All the other men involved in the airplanes—the armorers, the mechanics, the weather officers—had been waiting on the ground for seven or eight hours while we were away. They were a vital part of the team, but they saw nothing that happened, and they wanted to know!

And of course there were the other pilots. We were all feeling very emotional, whooping it up, in a tremendous state of excitation. It was partly the drug we were given—the benzedrine—but it was also because of what we had just gone through, and because we were back. We had made it.

We went around to each other, all talking at once, questioning one another, telling stories of what was seen or done.

Then the benzedrine wore off, and the beer wore off, and we went to bed exhausted. But I couldn't sleep, because the images were still going through my head. So I flew the mission again—re-living what I'd seen and done and reflecting on all the things that could have gone wrong. And if anybody was killed or missing, if one of us didn't come back, there was that to think about too. . . .

Suddenly I realized that the room was silent. Mr. Matsuda was looking at me, quietly and patiently, with no irritation. I did not know how long I had been lost in memories. He continued his story.

"On the day the war ended, I stripped the black-out curtains from my windows and, looking toward the heavens, I shouted, 'I have lived! I have lived!' I was grateful for my life and for the lives of my family.

"Our soldiers came home from the war to a country that was nearly destroyed. Almost every city had suffered unimaginable damage. For the first time in my memory, I could see Mount Fuji from Tokyo, nearly sixty miles away. No buildings stood to block the view. The population was homeless, without food—and without spirit. The glory of war had turned to the reality of horrendous defeat, humiliation, and death. Our children, our women, our elders could be seen scratching through the rubble for food and clothing. There was no electricity and hardly any fuel to cook what little rice was available.

"It was September when the first contingent of American soldiers arrived in Japan. No one knew how they would behave.

"It must have been a strange sight for your soldiers in the early days of the occupation. Only our oldest men dared venture into the streets. Our women and children were kept inside and at times hidden from sight, their sounds muffled for fear of being detected. For years the Japanese people had been told of the barbarous Americans: how they ate young children, raped and killed all women and terrorized the population! Our soldiers were told that if they became prisoners, their arms would be hacked off and the bones made into letter openers that would be sold in America.

"We always were told of their cruelty. We knew from our own long history, and the history of other nations, that the defeated would be subjected to severe punishment and treatment. This was the way of the conqueror. We were totally unprepared for the attitude of your occupation forces. They were not anything like we thought they would be. The soldiers were so tall, so well fed. And they were gentle. Our children were given food and candy almost from the first day of the occupation. Soup kitchens were set up and, gradually, all of our people were given food. It was the beginning of a new way of life for all of us, and it was made easier by the kindness of the American troops.

"The signing of the surrender treaty in Yokohama Bay was a day that signaled a complete change in the Japanese way of life. Shortly after the signing, Emperor Hirohito spoke on the radio for the very first time. All of Japan fell to its knees as he outlined what was expected of us. No matter what was asked by the occupying forces, we were to do it. We were to obey them as if it were he himself talking. Japan must be obedient to the laws established by the Americans.

" 'Our way of life will change.' he told us. 'All must accept this new life, as if I myself have ordained it. We must maintain our dignity and work hard to rebuild our cities, our country, our place in the world. I can assure you that we will be treated fairly by the American military forces. They have assured me that they will not interfere with our internal way of life.' "

Quietly I said, "Matsuda San, I was on that first fighter mission over Tokyo. I watched from the sky what you experienced on the ground."

Mr. Matsuda looked at me then closed his eyes. I fell silent, withdrew into myself. We sat in this tomb of silence for quite some time, thinking about what we had been talking about, what was happening in the room. I remember putting my hands over my eyes, and in the darkness, my thoughts turned to my childhood.

My sister and I often used to bring home stray kittens, lost dogs and wounded birds. My mother helped us feed them milk using eye droppers. From her and the animals, we learned about life, how precious it was. We tried to be as gentle with our charges as their mothers might. I thought about the Boy Scouts and remembered the Scout Oath. It began, "On my honor I will do my duty to God and my country, to obey the scout law." A scout is reverent, helpful, and the rest. The scouts taught me about nature, how to live in the woods, always to protect the environment, never to leave a fire without making sure it was out. And then I thought about April 7, 1945. How I had flown my P-51 over the home we were sitting in now, protecting the B-29s as they dropped their lethal loads, watching gleefully as the bombs exploded and the fires spread, thinking that the people below me were just "Japs"—my enemies.

It never occurred to me that a man like Sen might be on the ground hearing and feeling the bombs explode around him. He must have heard the cries of pain from the maimed, the cries of anguish from the injured and dying. It must have been terrible to live like that, day after day, unable to do anything but sit and wait for the bombers to return. How was it possible that my values had been altered so quickly, that I could enjoy a war as much as I did, that I could help kill thousands of people because my country said I should? I disliked myself intently at that moment. After what must have been only a few minutes, I opened my eyes and looked at my new friend, Sen Matsuda.

I thought, "Here I am in a foreign land, sitting with a man I have met only once, talking about the most profound experience of my life." We belonged to two cultures, two countries, which had been bitter enemies in our lifetimes. And now, in a suburb of Tokyo, we were talking about the past, about that war, the killing, feeling toward one another as old and loving friends. It was a moving experience.

Time was running out on our visit. Mr. Matsuda excused himself for a few minutes and returned dressed in a splendid brown suit with a dark shirt and light tie. We said our good-byes to Midori and Mrs. Matsuda, and walked to the taxi she had called. As we walked to the waiting cab, Sen donned a hat, took his walking stick in hand and joined us for the ride to the station. We were to spend a few more minutes together on the train. He was going to Hakone to attend his high school class reunion. As the train pulled into the Atami station, he stood up slowly and took my hand in his.

"I am sorry that we met so late in your trip, and so late in my life," he said. "But I am grateful that we have had even this little time to spend together. Please come back again soon."

The train stopped, he stepped off, turned, and stood waving as our train pulled out of the station.

Helene took my hand as we walked back to our seats. I was staring out of the window trying to cope with what we had heard, when Helene said, "I'm having a hard time keeping from crying."

"Me, too. I wonder why we met this man at this time and spent a day with him? I really wanted to hear about the war from a man his age. I just never expected anything like this to happen on this trip. I wonder how many more Sen's live here; lived here when I was flying over their country?"

That night I couldn't sleep. I was upset by the memories that had begun surfacing as Mr. Matsuda told about his experiences during the war. And the feelings—anger, hatred, fear! I remembered what I had felt about the Japanese. The rage within me at the time was genuine. Some of what I felt came from what my mother told me when I began dating.

"How would you feel if you found a man had entered our home and was molesting your sister?" she asked me.

"I would kill him," I replied.

"Well, just remember that the girl you are dating tonight might have a brother who feels the same about his sister as you feel about yours."

That is how I felt about the Japanese. They had invaded my home, my country, and I would have to make them pay. All of the stories we began to hear from Corrigidor and Bataan, the indignation fueled by American propaganda that depicted the Japanese as "monsters," all contributed to my hatred for an entire nation of people. Now I had to look at them, and at me, from a different perspective.

I got up from the bed and went outside for a walk. It seemed so bizarre. At the same time that I was having these horrible memories about war, I was here walking the streets of Tokyo, late at night, a foreigner, one of the only Caucasians on the streets, and I felt perfectly safe, more safe and comfortable, in fact, than I would feel in my own country. And these were the streets that we had bombed nearly forty years ago!

I thought of the fear that our attacks must have caused in the people. And now, I felt no fear. The people were truly warm, helpful, and unthreatening. Whenever we needed help during our travels, we were directed to our destination by attentive strangers who made us feel welcome. We were always treated politely and courteously.

It was strange, I thought, that I felt no anger towards the Japanese people. But I was angry and I didn't know why. "It is appalling," I thought. "We keep repeating the same scenario over and over again only in different places with different people." I walked for hours before I returned to my hotel, feeling somewhat better, resolving nothing, my anger abated.

Helene had been worried by my absence. When I returned she asked me what was wrong.

"Nothing. I just couldn't sleep."

She knew that there was much more but did not press me further. She sensed my discomfort and anger, but she respected my silence. The next day we went to Kyoto.

CHAPTER
FOUR

Discovering Japan

HELENE AND I were anxiously looking forward to seeing the gardens and temple buildings of Kyoto that we had seen only in pictures. Our guide book listed all of the shrines in the area as well as the best time to view them. It was autumn and the leaves were beginning to change. We left the hotel, had the doorman call a taxi and I told the driver *"Arashiyama."* I repeated it two or three times before the doorman leaned into the cab and said *"Arashiyama."*

"Ah so, Arashiyama," the driver repeated and pulled away.

Helene looked at me and laughed, "I thought you learned the language."

I had studied Japanese for four months before we left San Diego. "I thought so, too," I replied. "Didn't I say the same thing they said?"

We drove along a fast-flowing river for thirty minutes, then across a bridge where the driver stopped his taxi and said *"Arashiyama."*

According to the guide books, this is one of the most beautiful areas of Kyoto—both in the spring at cherry blossom time and in the fall for the brilliant display of nature's many colors. We were not disappointed. We walked along the lake, viewing the gardens, feeling the solitude one feels with nature; in spite of the fact that it seemed every schoolchild in Japan was also out there, surrounding us! The approach to the gardens was blocked by photographers lining up high school students, to take their class pictures.

As noon approached we began to look for a restaurant to eat lunch. All were crowded with students. In one we spotted two empty seats next to two girls, aged about eighteen, and, the host asked if we would sit next to them. They both smiled shyly, hiding their smiles behind their hands so we would not see their teeth.

I said "*Konichiwa*." (Good afternoon.)

They said "Hello," (which came out "Herro"!), and we all laughed.Their lunch ended sooner than ours and they left, smiling and waving over their shoulders as they looked back at us.

Helene and I finished our *udon* (noodles) soon after, paid the check and left the restaurant to continue sightseeing. Neither of us expected to see our two table-mates again. However, they were standing a few feet from the entrance door, obviously waiting for us to appear. They bowed slightly as we approached them, and one girl said, "My name is Takako, and this is my friend Hisako. We are students in Hatoyama High School. We are on a school trip. We visited Nara, Hiroshima, and now, Kyoto."

"Yes," joined in Hisako, shyly. "Our teacher has asked us to speak to foreigners we meet and ask them a few questions. May we ask you our questions?"

"Of course," I replied.

They handed each of us a sheet of paper that read, "Our school class is studying peace. We have just returned from Hiroshima, where the atomic bomb was dropped in 1945. Over 200,000 people were killed by the bombs. I want to live in peace and I want my children to live in peace. Please tell us what you think about peace, and please draw an X on the above map to show us where you live."

Unexpectedly, tears came into my eyes, Helene's as well, as we wrote our answers.

I hadn't expected to speak about war among the natural beauties of Kyoto. But here I was forced to think about it again by the daughters of my enemy. On their sheets I wrote about flying a P-51 over Japan many times in World War II, and that I longed for a peaceful world. Helene's message was similar. "I was a young girl when the war started," she wrote, "and about your age when the war ended. I read about Hiroshima in a book by an American author and I remember how sad I felt for anyone who experienced the horrors of war. I, too, want to live in peace and to see my children and their children live in peace as well. We must never allow war to occur again." The mood of our afternoon shifted dramatically as our attention was drawn to the high school students and their project on peace in the world. After we filled in their paper, they handed us a post card with their names, addresses, and the message of peace written on it.

A few months later, I sent Hisako and Takako an

article I had written; the story of my experiences in the war. In time I received the following letter. It came from Tamio Yanagisma, Takako and Hisako's English teacher.

"After we returned from Kyoto last November, I collected fifty-two messages my students had received. I told them that your messages were the most impressive ones we had received. I made a handout of your messages and all 280 students in the class read them. So I was extremely happy when you wrote to my students and enclosed your article. I was not only happy but very moved. Your experience in the war was severe and sad. But now you have discovered that the Japanese are peace-loving people. I was caught by the deep emotions of your story and asked my students to make a booklet, translated by them and me, for the rest of the school. I will send you one when it is completed. A lot of thanks to both of you for giving my students a precious and unforgettable memory on their school trip."

That first week in Japan created confusion and emotions within me that were difficult to deal with. I hadn't expected the welcome by those we encountered or the serenity and beauty we saw. Although I remembered how green the countryside was in the spring and summer of 1945 when I was strafing airfields or trains, I was not prepared for the openness or friendliness of the people we encountered or the stillness I found in the surroundings. Even in Tokyo, with all the noise and bustle, we found small parks and shrines that reverberated in silence.

Back in Tokyo, the concierge in our hotel recommended we see the Festival of the Cranes at a nearby temple. "You are fortunate. The festival is this afternoon. The temple grounds are beautiful this time of year and the Crane Festival is famous all over Japan. Many dancers will imitate the graceful movements of the crane in their mating rites. The crane is a symbolic bird to the Japanese. It is said that the Emperor is the voice of the crane and the dance is a dance of life. We also believe that the crane is the bird that carries our souls to heaven when we die."

"Is the festival far?" Helene asked.

"No, no. Just a few minutes walk. Come, I will show you the way."

The three of us walked to the street in front of the hotel. The concierge pointed, and said, "Two blocks that way, then left three blocks. You will see lots of people there."

The sidewalks were crowded with people, the streets filled with cars and taxi cabs. Somehow all seemed orderly. I don't remember hearing any horns blowing. There were no cars in the road on the approach to the temple. The street, instead, was filled with thirty or forty men wearing papier mache feathers, weaving, emulating a gyrating bird, as they approached the temple stairs.

As we neared the shrine, I immediately noticed two elderly men in uniform—Japanese soldiers— alongside the steps. One was without arms and had a cup strapped around his neck, for passers-by to toss coins into. The other was legless, sitting on his stumps on a blanket. I was startled for the moment and felt a powerful urge to approach them, an almost overwhelming desire to talk to these soldiers.

It was the strangest feeling, one I had never felt before. I looked at them with pity for their wounds. But there was more. I knew I would feel better if I could talk to them, but I wanted them to talk to me as well. I felt the need to talk about the war with someone who had fought on the other side.

Looking at the crippled veterans, I felt the shame and embarrassment they must have been feeling. Begging is not a dignified pastime for anyone, let alone soldiers, Japanese or American.

Of course, I didn't speak to them. I didn't even go near them. I dropped a few coins into one of the tin boxes and turned aside.

Then, quite suddenly, it struck me. These were the first live Japanese soldiers I had ever seen! Almost instantly I was back on Iwo Jima. The last Japanese soldier I had seen was a dead officer in a cave.

It is common practice to pick up a few souvenirs during wartime: an enemy helmet or bayonet, a flag, part of a uniform. One afternoon on Iwo, a few of us put on our helmets, took a Jeep, and drove to an American-held area where I knew a staff sergeant.

"Captain Yellin," he said, when we pulled up. "Do you want to see a cave that we've finally captured? We've been trying to take it for days."

"Yes," we all replied eagerly.

We thought we might pick up some souvenirs to take home. And we wanted to see the dead Japs. We wanted to feel that, to know that. Part of being a soldier on Iwo Jima was to go see dead Japs where they were killed. For me, it was a way to at least see the results of somebody else's fighting. As a pilot, I never saw the results of mine.

The sergeant led us past some trees, where we saw the burned, twisted bodies of Japanese soldiers who had been caught by flame-throwers; nothing more was left of them than black shadows in the charred branches.

We had to be careful entering the cave. Because the Japanese knew that Americans would examine the dead bodies for souvenirs, they had a policy of mining their dead. They would attach bombs to the bodies, or bury bombs or mortar shells nearby and stretch thin, almost invisible trip wires between bodies, attached to a belt or belt loop. When the Americans went through the area, they would set off the bombs. The Japanese killed a lot of people this way.

The sergeant led us into a still-smoking entrance way that was partially blocked by a dead soldier, a young officer. The body must have been lying there for some time because the smell in the cave was horrible. The soldier's face was full of maggots. I reached down and pulled the belt on his pants to move the body so that we could pass into the cave. The belt almost went right through the body. I shuddered and let go of it.

Next to the body lay a photograph of a man in full-dress uniform and a little girl—obviously the young officer and his daughter. She was wearing a white dress, her eyes bright under a dark head of hair. Their faces were serious and composed, as the Japanese always prefer to be in pictures.

Despite the almost unbearable stench, we carefully walked deeper inside the cave. I saw a small wooden box and opened it. Among other things it contained a ceremonial knife, wrapped in a piece of cloth.

"That's a *hara-kiri* knife," my Marine friend said. "Do you want to keep it?" I did.

After I got back to my foxhole that night I couldn't sleep. I couldn't even close my eyes. And in later years, when I had recurring dreams of the war, I was always in that cave with the dead Japanese body. Night after night I saw the picture of the man with his daughter—that, and the maggot-filled eyes of the dead soldiers piled up for burial.

I put the *hara-kiri* knife in my foot locker where it stayed until I took it with me on my return home after the war. That, and a blood-stained Japanese flag that I took from a dead soldier's body, were the only mementos of the war that I kept.

Of course, the real souvenirs of the war, which I had stored in my mind and carried around with me always, were my memories, those images. Nobody knew about them. I never talked about them to anyone. But I saw these pictures almost every day for years.

CHAPTER
FIVE

Kenrokuen

HIDA TAKAYAMA is a mountain town famous for its 600-year-old thatched roof farm village. On our first morning there, we got lost. We were staying at a *ryokan* near the restored village. We walked into the small village and could not remember how to get back to our inn from town.

There were groups of Japanese students everywhere we traveled, sightseeing and having their pictures taken by classmates or by professional photographers. All wore school uniforms; even the youngest ones, those in kindergarten and first grade. They would typically stare at Helene and me, hold up their fingers in a V, and grin as we pointed our camera in their direction.

The older girls sometimes shyly approached us (never singly; always in pairs or more) and asked us to pose with them. They laughed and giggled, holding their hands over their mouths in a delightful gesture of modesty as they thanked us.

We approached a group of five high school students for directions. The students, all boys, huddled together for a moment, then asked us to follow them.

They all started talking at once, in English, and even shouted to their teacher that they were taking the *gai-jin* (foreigners) to the village and would meet the class at the bus sometime later.

They were anxious to impress us with their knowledge of America, their language skills, and their pride in the village buildings. When we passed an ice-cream stand, we stopped and bought them ice cream, which, they pronounced, "aisucuremu." They, in turn, bought a small souvenir for Helene—a set of minia-ture Japanese dolls which she still has, nearly a decade later. The boys even paid for a ticket to an exhibit they wanted us to see.

With all the stops and the animated conversa-tions, the short walk back to our inn took two hours. I couldn't imagine approaching five high school stu-dents in America and then following them around for two hours in a strange city! I am not even sure that I would have been so gracious and helpful to foreigners when I was younger, and I'm not proud of that. And these were the children and the grandchildren of the people I had hated.

Our travels also took us to the Kenrokuen, one of Japan's three most famous landscape gardens, situated in Kanazawa, capital of the whole Hokuriku (seacoast) area, seven hours from Tokyo by train.

To the Japanese, a perfect garden consists of six elements: water, size, serenity, space, careful arrange-ment, and appearance. Kenrokuen has all of these ele-ments, blended in exquisite beauty.

Helene and I spent two days there in the misty rains of late October. We walked on stone pathways through the pine trees, across streams and small lakes with garden islands.

From the front gate, we heard the sound of running water under the small, stone bridge at the entrance and were immediately enchanted. The leaves were changing color, and the gardens were ablaze with red and gold, interspersed with green pine trees. It was early in the morning, rain had fallen the night before and a light fog hung in the air. It seemed as if we were the only people in the entire garden. As we walked across the bridge and entered the garden, Helene stopped, and, overcome with the silence and the exquisite vista, tears forming in her eyes, said, "I have never ever felt or seen such beauty."

Every tree in Kenrokuen is carefully tended and has a life unto itself. It doesn't get lost, as in a forest, but each is cut and pruned to bring out its full beauty and individuality. The park is over one hundred acres in extent, and gravel paths lead in all directions. A beautiful lake spread out through the park, with many islands in it and huge stepping stones leading out to them.

The garden had space, and beautiful colors from the changing leaves. It had water, both flowing and still. It had serenity. And best of all, because of the weather, it had solitude and quiet. There was no one there.

While we were walking in the park, Helene told me something that, she said, had been increasingly on her mind during the trip.

"You know, Robert would love this place."

"You mean these gardens?"

"Yes, he would love the gardens. But I'm talking about Japan. He would like the stillness and the beauty that we have felt and seen."

Helene and I met on a blind date on Good Friday, 1949, became engaged on May 30th and were married on October 22. She was only nineteen years old when we were married, I was twenty-five. Our first son, David was born thirteen months later, followed shortly by Steven, Michael and Robert, all before we celebrated our tenth anniversary. Helene and I always had a meaningful, close relationship. I can't remember a time in our lives that she wasn't there for me or the children.

She has been my guide to a richer life. When she and Steven began practicing Transcendental Meditation in August 1975, I resisted her urging to join in meditation until April 1976 when I learned TM. It has been one of the many unifying experiences we have shared in our life together. As we have grown older and our children moved into their own careers, we have become even closer. I trust her judgment in everything, yet I had never told her about my experiences as a fighter pilot on Iwo Jima or over Japan. She never asked and I never offered.

Shortly after we moved to California in 1976, Helene visited Warrens, an oriental antique store in Laguna Beach, with a friend. That night she told me how much she was affected by what she had seen. "I can't explain the feeling that came over me," she said. "The aesthetics, the lines of the architecture, the shape of the pottery, the screens—everything I saw fascinated me. There seemed to be a connection."

That was the beginning of our small collection of Japanese artifacts and books on gardens. She spent countless hours reading and looking at pictures of Japanese art. Through her influence, we came to own several lovely Japanese antiques, a beautiful screen, some calligraphy and pottery.

Robert is the youngest of our four sons. David, our oldest son, introduced us to the mood and the sounds of the sixties when he brought Bob Dylan records into our home. In time, we learned to enjoy the music and the poetry, but it wasn't easy. Steven, Michael and Robert all collected the music of the day as well. From our sons we learned a new language, new philosophies. David began his search for life's meaning at eighteen when he began studying Eastern religions.

As our children were growing, they searched and found a spirituality far beyond what I knew. Helene seemed to sense more of a spiritual feeling in Robert than I did and felt he would resonate with Japan. She often followed her intuition about what she thought her sons would like to read, to see and experience. She was rarely wrong.

"There is a lot here to interest him," she said. "I think we should offer Rob a trip to Japan as a graduation present."

Robert is an unusual young man, someone who has always been very deep and sensitive. I was learning that a spiritual influence permeates the Japanese culture: a love for nature, a sense of oneness, respect, and awe. The thought of my son visiting Japan never crossed my mind. I didn't respond for a few minutes and finally agreed, "Why not, we can afford it." I had enjoyed my visit so far and was beginning to see Japan in a different light. We decided to suggest it to Robert as soon as we returned to the States.

CHAPTER SIX

Robert's Trip

A FEW DAYS LATER we boarded a 747 at Narita Airport for the return to San Diego. For most of our flight home, I was deep in thought, and for many days afterwards, as well. I had visions of the dead Japanese on Iwo Jima intermixed with the peace and serenity of the temples and the gardens of Kenrokuen, the warm hospitality of the Japanese inns, and the smiles and bows of the men, women, and children we had met.

All the people we had killed in the war were no longer faceless "Japs" and "enemies." Now they were starting to come to life. I saw them as people—the crippled veterans at the shrine, and that refined gentleman, Mr. Matsuda. I saw them on the streets with their families. I spoke to them and they to me. I rode on trains with them, sat down to meals with them and became friends.

The deep, distressful impressions of my youth were challenged by a whole series of new and very positive impressions. I felt my heart open to this country and to these people. But the agonizing memories were still there.

In my determination to learn more about Japan
and her people, I joined a Japanese golf organization
at Torrey Pines Golf Course and played every week
with the same group, mostly executives of Japanese
firms. Numata San, Uchiyama San, and Kagawa San
became my friends and teachers. These young executives of Japanese companies in San Diego played golf
at every opportunity. They did not earn enough
money to play in Japan where golf is expensive yet
they could play in San Diego for a mere eight dollars
a round. It was quite possible that they were sons of
Japanese soldiers, however, I never asked them nor did
they ask me about the war.

I never enjoyed playing golf with a group of people more than with my Japanese friends. They were all
good golfers, excellent competitors, and fine sports-
men. Regardless of how they played, they never lost
their sense of humor or composure. As I got to know
them better, I saw they had an appreciation for life
which was similar to what I had observed in my own
sons.

Our son, Robert, had a Japanese friend, Hiro,
who owned a sushi bar near San Diego State
University. We went there frequently, learned to
appreciate the Japanese delicacies and the rituals that
accompany eating Japanese food. We also added to
our small collection of Japanese art and antiques.

For most of my adult life I had only looked at life
from an American perspective. I wanted Robert to
experience something more, but I thought that if
offered a trip to Japan he might refuse. And I really
wanted him to go there. I couldn't put my finger on

the real reason, but I felt it was more than just a grad-uation present. Perhaps it was an affirmation of what I had learned about the country. Or, could there be a hidden, deeper reason?

In Japan I saw a cohesiveness that had always eluded me. Although I was Jewish, I had never experi-enced the closeness associated with belonging to a temple, or living in a Jewish neighborhood. We moved often, my father had little religious leanings; my mother had been raised an orphan in a variety of faiths. She always insisted that I had to try harder, do better than others because I was Jewish, but I didn't believe that while I was young.

Anti-Semitism flourished in our country in the 1930s and came into my life when I was twelve years old. We lived in Hillside, New Jersey where my fami-ly rented a house on Bond Street. Our house was next to an empty lot that was used for baseball in the sum-mer and football in the fall. There were enough kids on our block to field teams for every sport. I played second base on the baseball team and was the quarter-back in football. In the summer of 1936 all that ended. I awoke one day and found my house covered with Nazi Swastikas and "Jew" written all over the garage. From that day I was marked, and the guys I had played with stopped calling. I heard them refer to me as a "cowardly Jew like all the rest of them." Even though there were rumblings about Nazis in Irvington, the town next to us, we never expected anything like that to happen to us.

When the war started I was determined to be as good, if not better, at my job than anyone else. I wanted to prove that we Jews could fight. Even though we knew a little about what was happening to the Jews in Europe, I only wanted to fight against the people that attacked my country. The Japanese were my enemy!

As our children grew older I felt the need to give them the religious education I never had. We joined a synagogue where I took an active role, and they studied. Our first three sons had no choice in the matter. They went to Hebrew school and were Bar Mitzvah. But Robert was different. He never liked being told what to do and demonstrated this in many ways as a young man. At twelve he refused to continue Hebrew School and didn't want to be Bar Mitzvah. I didn't argue. At fourteen he asked if it was too late to do it. We found out that it could be done at any age, so he was Bar Mitzvah at fourteen. His independence continued throughout high school and college. Robert always worked to have spending money and, at eighteen, moved into his own apartment.

He adopted a cat and named him Biko after the South African activist who died in jail. He visited a ninety-year-old invalid in a nursing home three days a week, seeing to it that the old man had enough to read and sometimes just kept him company. He worked at Tower Records near San Diego State College. His extensive record collection was always circulating; his small house was always filled with friends. He never asked us for anything and often refused what we wanted to give him. Yet, he always maintained a certain presence, a dignity and sensitivity to others.

When Helene and I offered him a trip between

his junior and senior year at college, he couldn't decide between Europe or Japan. Then I read about a six week "home stay" program in the travel section of the *Los Angeles Times*. The trip was sponsored by the YMCA in Los Angeles and Kiddy College in Japan. When I told Robert the details, he accepted enthusiastically.

Robert left for Japan in July of 1984 for a six-week stay with a family in Mishima where Kiddy College is located. It is about one hundred miles by train from Tokyo. He was met at the station by Mr. Yas Takesue, the President of Kiddy and the sponsor of the home stay program. Mr. Takesue accompanied Robert to the home of the Yamamoto family, his hosts. In his second letter home, he referred to the Yamamotos as "my Japanese family."

Robert spent three weeks with the Yamamoto family visiting local places of interest, shrines, and temples. Near the end of the trip he was awarded a Japanese flag and walking pole for climbing Mount Fuji.

When he showed the flag to me upon his return to San Diego, I was startled. How incredible, I thought, this symbol of the rising sun was painted on the sides and wings of the airplanes I had shot at over Japan. This symbol of the Japanese military was given to my son as a prize for his victorious ascent of a mountain—it was identical to the flag I had taken from a dead Japanese soldier on Iwo Jima.

During his senior year at San Diego State College, Robert corresponded regularly with Mr.

Takesue, the sponsor of the Japanese home stay program. When he graduated he thought about spending a year teaching English in Japan before settling on a career. Thinking this a good idea, he applied to several universities and also to Mr. Takesue's school.

In August Mr. Takesue offered Robert a position for one year. Robert accepted, but expressed apprehension about his teaching abilities. Mr. Takesue reassured him:

"All of our students have already had English in school and simply want to polish their conversational skills. They will help you with your Japanese and you, most assuredly, will help them with their English. Most of our teachers are college graduates, like you, who want to experience Japan for a year or two."

Robert was delighted.

"Some of the teachers," Takesue told him, "simply stay for one or two years. But a few have met and married other teachers. Some have even married Japanese women and remained in our country."

In 1984 Robert returned to Japan and moved in again with the Yamamotos.

CHAPTER
SEVEN

Meeting Takako

IN MARCH 1987 we received a letter from Robert urging us to visit him in Japan. He wanted us to see his new home and his new life. We went in May.

I had a good feeling when I saw Robert standing on the platform as our train arrived at Mishima. He looked like he belonged there, even though he was much taller than the Japanese men. He had grown a full beard again and his hair was long and curly brown.

I had been looking forward to this trip to Japan for many reasons. I suspected that Robert would not return to America to live, and I wanted to see if I could accept that.

Mishima is at the head of the Izu Peninsula, a favorite tourist area for the Japanese. Not far from Hakone, with its many spas, a large lake, and extraordinary views of Mount Fuji, Izu is a Mecca for those seeking a change from the fast pace of the city. The train station at Mishima offers the traveler a splendid view of Mount Fuji from the platform. Connecting trains, buses, and cars take visitors down the peninsula to a variety of tourist areas.

Heda, a one-hour ride by car, is famous for the

world's largest crabs. Caught in several thousand feet of water, they sometimes reach twelve to fourteen feet long. Later in our trip, Mrs. Yamamoto invited us to dine on a Heda crab whose legs were each six feet long. Sixteen of us had dinner from that one crab.

The Izu Peninsula points due south from the mainland, almost like an arrow pointed toward Iwo Jima. I flew that imaginary line on my first mission over Japan, crossing Hara, a section of the city of Numazu, that would be significant in Robert's future.

Robert, Helene, and I drove nearly 1600 kilometers (about 1000 miles) in his small car, entirely at Robert's expense. He took us to an elegant *ryokan* (Japanese inn) in Shuzenji. Our room had a balcony overlooking a fast-running river, and cherry blossoms filled our picture window. Further on in our travels, we had dinner and stayed overnight in a 200-year-old farm house owned by one of his students. In the morning when we awoke, we could see snow-capped Mount Fuji in the distance. Robert escorted us to famous shrines and gardens, and whenever I offered to pay for something, or to buy him something, he always said, "You've done enough. Now it's my turn."

We traveled around the countryside for two weeks, and Helene kept saying to me, "Robert is going to marry a Japanese woman. I just know it."

Whenever I thought about the possibility of Robert marrying a Japanese woman, I wondered if I could accept such an event. Slowly I had begun to accept the Japanese as people, even though the memories of war surfaced from time to time. But my family? I was beginning to understand Japan, the culture, but a son married to a Japanese? I just didn't know.

Robert chauffeured us in his small Japanese car, which, with three *gaijins* and several weeks' worth of luggage, was quite crowded. I was not at all comfortable driving on the "wrong" side of the road, and the narrow width of the streets created several close calls. Whenever a bus or truck approached, one had to give way, usually accompanied by a beep of the horn, a nod of the head, and a wave of the hand. Robert laughed as I jammed my foot on a non-existent brake.

"This part of Mishima was completely untouched by the American bombers," he explained. "The roads didn't need to be rebuilt. This is one of the older parts of town, and the roads are as narrow as when they were used by wagons and carts." Robert didn't know that I had strafed the rail station and boats in the harbor nearby.

Robert had established himself in his own tiny apartment, about ten minutes from the station. On the second night of our visit, he took us to meet his Japanese family. The Yamamoto's lived about thirty minutes away. On the way, Robert described the family and their home.

"Their house is large by Japanese standards," he said. "It's a hundred years old and has been remodeled several times. It was owned by Mr. Yamamoto's father. When his father died, ownership went to him, the eldest son."

Robert said that Mrs. Yamamoto spent most of her time in the kitchen, cooking for her family and two Japanese boarders. Tea and sweets were always offered to friends and family when they stopped in to visit.

"As in most Japanese families, she's in charge of just about everything, except the actual earning of money. On pay day, Mr. Yamamoto gives her the check, and she allocates a portion for savings and then spreads the rest into accounts for food, education, clothing, and vacation.

"The oldest son is Takuya. He's in high school, and he's quite proficient in English. After I had been around awhile, he wrote a paper about the impact of having a foreigner living under the same roof. I think I wrote to you about this."

He had, and in his letter he had quoted Takuya's remarks. "At first," the boy had written, "talking with Bob in English was a pleasure, and indeed he was a good person for my English conversation training. But now I feel he is one of my family. And I've got to think that we are the same human beings in spite of the differences in languages, customs, colors of hair, eyes, and skin."

As I recalled the letter, I realized that I was learning the same lesson about our common humanity.

"Erina, the only daughter, is a typically happy, giggly, teenager," said Robert. "The moment she comes home from school she changes from her school uniform into clothes that any teenager in San Diego might wear. But her attitude remains completely Japanese. The first thing she does is her homework. Then, as it starts to get dark, she helps in the preparation of the evening meal. And she does all this without any prompting from her mother."

When Robert told Mrs. Yamamoto that he was

going home to be best man at his brother Michael's wedding, she asked him to take Erina with him to America. Helene and I were quite surprised at the time that the Yamamotos would entrust a young girl, who did not speak English, to a stranger for such a long trip. Robert assured us that in their eyes she was not traveling with a stranger but with her "brother."

"The youngest member of the family," Robert continued, "is Koji. He has also come to think of me as a brother but a *gaijin* big brother, a foreigner. We often wrestle on the floor, much as I did at home with my own brothers when I was younger.

"One of the great things about living with the Yamamotos is that it gives me the feeling of family that I enjoyed so much at home in America," Robert said. "And of course, it has made learning Japanese a lot easier.

"When I arrived last year, it was their first experience of having a visitor, other than a native Japanese, staying with them. We all carried dictionaries and everyone helped me with the proper words and expressions needed to speak correctly and politely. The differences in language, and in culture, took some time to overcome. Mrs. Yamamoto had to tell me things like, 'Take off your shoes before stepping on the floor,' and 'Don't use soap in the bathtub,' things that are as basic and obvious to the Japanese as 'Flush the toilet after you use it' would be to us. There really are some big differences in the conduct of daily life here."

"Did people give you a hard time for being different?" Helene asked. I laughed, remembering how he had stood out at the train station.

"Westerners are perceived as quite different," he said. "One day a little cousin, visiting the Yamamotos, became frightened when she saw me with my full beard and actually ran out of the room crying! I was probably the first foreigner she had ever seen. There are very few non-Japanese people living in rural Japan."

When we arrived at the Yamamotos, Robert greeted the first person that we met as Obaasan. He explained, "This is Mr. Yamamoto's mother, whom we all address as 'grandmother.' Obaasan has her garden in the rear of the house, where she spends most of her day tending her vegetables."

In her mid-seventies, Obaasan was a tiny woman, her back bent over like almost all elderly Japanese women. Yet she moved with great vigor, and her unlined face made her look much younger than her years.

"When I lived here, I shared the wing of the house where Obaasan lives, and we grew closer and closer as the months went by," Robert told us. "As I became more proficient in Japanese, she shared her life story with me, partly by singing folk songs." In his letters home, Robert referred to her as "my Japanese grandmother."

Obaasan invited us to have tea with her, and as we sat together she explained the Japanese concept of "inside" and "outside."

"When I was young," Obaasan began, with Robert translating, "I learned about living in a clean manner from my mother: Never bring anything from the outside to the inside. Outside is the *soto* world; it is dirty. Inside, the *uchi* world, is clean. Leave your shoes in the hall, clean your mouth when you enter, wash the dirt from your hands, then enter the *uchi*. Your home is inside, your schoolroom is inside, your office is inside, and you must keep them all clean.

"When we bathed at night we all washed the dirt from our bodies outside of the tub, then entered the inside world of the clean water to relax our minds and our spirits.

"In school," Obaasan continued, "we learned to be responsible for our desk; to leave it each day as if we might never come back. Our classroom was our inside world, too, and each of us had to do a daily chore: serving milk, or cleaning the room so it would be ready for the next day. The entire school was an inside world as well, so each student had an added responsibility to each of their other classmates. In that way, we learned to keep the entire school clean, both inside and outside."

"It's still the same, actually," Robert interjected. "Modern schoolchildren have the same duties. Most Japanese schools, if not all of them, are cared for entirely by the students and teachers. There are no janitors to clean up. Imagine how differently American students would treat their schools if they had to take care of them!"

"As we grew older," Obaasan continued, "our responsibilities got bigger and more important. No one, for example, would ever think of letting down their schoolmates, so everyone did the best job he could. Our school became a second home to us and we took great pride in making it the best we knew how."

At this point, we were called to the main part of the house. The Yamamoto children were setting a long, low table in a large room off the kitchen, where we would eat dinner when Mr. Yamamoto arrived home.

I soon discovered that Mr. Yamamoto is a calligrapher, in his early forties, thin and quite small. He was quick to smile and had a lovely sense of humor. When I admired one of his framed calligraphies, he took it off the wall and gave it to me. "Presento" he said. I was embarrassed and tried to refuse it, but to no avail. I learned that the custom in Japan is "admiration leads to possession." Robert took us to the homes of a number of fine artists and potters but I never again admired a man's work to his face.

As we returned to Robert's apartment, we turned off the highway, and the road divided to go around a large tree. "What a beautiful tree!" I remarked. Robert looked over at me and smiled, "I have a story to tell about that tree, Dad.

"I used to travel the twelve kilometers between Kiddy College in Mishima and my home here in Numazu, every day by bus. I spent many hours waiting for the bus under that tree. In the winter its branches protected me from the wind and the rain, and in the summer they offered shade and protection from the sun. I came to feel a lot of love for it.

"I learned from the Yamamotos that the tree has been standing there for more than two hundred years and is now officially protected by the town. As time went by I found myself looking forward to seeing the tree, as one looks forward to seeing a good friend. Often, when I touched it, I felt energy surge through my body, and a peaceful feeling would come over me. I thought this kind of odd and kept it to myself.

"Once, when I had a minor decision to make, I verbalized it under the tree. The options rolled through my mind, and the decision I reached worked out well. I found it comforting, from then on, to think things through while standing under the tree. I started to think of it as 'my special tree,' and began to refer to it that way.

"In Japan, I learned, there are many such trees: places where one goes to find solitude, to withdraw into oneself, and feel the energy of life that surges through this ancient land."

Robert became quiet for a moment, perhaps wondering how much to say.

"You remember that I wrote to you about the Australian fellow Richard, another English teacher I met here in Mishima? He and I sometimes seek out this energy, at the Rotenburo Onsen (outdoor bath) at Shuzenji. The Rotenburo is an ancient, outdoor hot spring that has been in use for over eight hundred years. The water comes from deep within the earth and rises next to a fast-moving stream.

"We often meet there late in the evening and soak in the 120°F water. Sometimes we speak, and sometimes we just share the moment in silence. Sitting in this rocky pool of hot water, as others have done for so many years, gives me a sense of timelessness and continuity. I like that feeling a lot.

"The mountains, the trees, the cherry blossoms,

the autumn leaves, Mount Fuji . . . all have this indescribable sense of tomorrow and of yesterday. For generation after generation, these places have been looked upon as reverent and holy."

The more he revealed his feelings to us, the more we understood why he had chosen to continue living there. How right Helene had been about Robert! She knew he would love the country. As we traveled with him and he shared his perceptions and understandings with us, our own appreciation of Japanese culture steadily increased.

Helene and I met Robert's girl friend, Takako, on our second night in Japan. She was due at Robert's at six for dinner. That morning, when Robert told us she would be coming, he described their first meeting.

"It was six months after I began working at Kiddy College," he said. "I noticed her on her first day at work. She was cute and cheerful, and I asked her to have lunch with me. We went to a small coffee shop in Mishima called Strawberry Fields and spent the entire time absorbed in pleasant conversation.

"From that day on we dated regularly. She was shy, intelligent, quite serious, and had a special presence about her that I didn't see in other Japanese girls of her age. We had so many things in common— music, love of nature, her interest in learning more about teaching, especially English—things like that.

"In the beginning of our relationship we did a lot of driving. Takako had a car and I didn't, so we would drive around the Izu peninsula and explore different areas around here. There's not much to do in Mishima and Numazu, so we would talk for hours in coffee shops. She told me about her family, I told her about mine. Sometimes it was hard to communicate, because my Japanese wasn't very good, and Takako's English wasn't much better than my Japanese. But I had a good feeling about her, so we have continued to see each other."

When Takako arrived at Robert's apartment promptly at six, fresh from the hair dresser, Helene was getting dressed, and Robert had not yet come home. Takako sat on the floor opposite me on a cushion. I knew this was a difficult moment for her, and for me as well. I wanted to make it easy for her, she seemed so shy and uncomfortable.

In an attempt to ease her obvious discomfort, I said, "We're really pleased to be here, and to meet you. I don't know what Robert's plans are, but I want you to know that whatever Robert decides to do, including living in Japan, will be all right with me.

"I have many concerns, however, about my ability to accept a serious relationship with a Japanese woman. I flew over your country several times as a young man. Many of my friends were killed. I have not resolved all of that in my mind yet. As a father, I will not stand in the way of my son's decisions. But as an American, I am not sure I can accept his decision whole heartedly. I also don't know anything about your father and his feelings about Robert, about America, about the war."

Takako did not respond, just nodded her head as I spoke, concentrating on my words. Looking back, as I write this, it must have sounded quite ominous to her. I do find that I took a lot for granted, without really knowing what their plans were.

I continued, "I was born in February of 1924. When was your father born?"

Perhaps over-eager to please, Takako said that he had been born in the same month of the same year. We found out later that he was actually born almost a year later in December 1924.

I asked, "Was he in the war?"

"He never talked about it much, but I know he was in the army in China for three years."

She was young and pretty, with dark eyes and thick black hair. But she was quite shy. She rarely spoke unless we said something first. Robert called her "Taco," much to her evident annoyance (Taco means "octopus" in Japanese!). They seemed at ease with each other.

I wanted to know more about her father. Did he know of their relationship? Did he approve? When I asked her if her parents had met Robert she said, "No, not yet."

When she left that evening, I gave her a bottle of brandy to give to her father as a gift. Towards the end of our trip, she gave me a canister of Japanese tea, a gift from him. This was significant to me, as an opening that might be helpful to Robert if and when he was to meet Takako's parents. It seemed to be an acknowledgment that he had accepted my gift and then reciprocated.

Although no one had said anything, I suspected that there was a marriage in their future. In that first meeting, I had asked Takako, "How do you keep busy, besides your job?"

She quietly said, "I'm making plans for my wedding." As she said this, I fell into a well of silence.

CHAPTER
EIGHT

Dilemma

BEFORE OUR TRIP to Japan to visit Robert, we knew that he had begun to collect Bizen pottery. Helene and I had come across some Bizen Ware in a shop in La Jolla. The owners, she Japanese, he American, were unable to continue importing Japanese merchandise and were going out of business. We asked about the Bizen *sake* jars and cups and were told that they were made by a famous Japanese potter and were not for sale. We explained that we had a son in Japan who loved Bizen pottery and we wanted to give them to him for his birthday. They became excited that their favorite pieces of pottery would be in the hands of an appreciative owner and set a price. They told us that they wanted the new owner to be a collector who could appreciate the distinction of Bizen ware. When we gave Robert the boxed set of sake jars and cups on his birthday, we told him how we had acquired them.

As had become his custom, he looked up the potters mark and called the Isezaki home in Bizen. This led to a visit and the beginning of a friendship.

Robert told Mrs. Isezaki that Helene and I were

in Japan, and she suggested we visit them in Bizen. "I would like to meet your parents," she told Robert, "they are the ones who made our pottery take a long journey from our home, to America, and now, back to Japan."

We accepted her offer and spent two days in Bizen meeting many of Robert's friends. Pottery has been made in Bizen for one thousand years. At the turn of the century there were only forty potters in the town. They shared kilns built into the nearby hills and helped each other in the firing twice a year. Today there are about four hundred potters in the area.

Before visiting the Isezaki's home, we went to Mr. Yokoyama's, our "teapot potter's" shop. We had been using one of his Bizen teapots and cups for several years. Mr. Yokoyama is the youngest of the potters we met, under thirty and a rising star. He and Robert shared a few "professional" moments together while Helene and I inspected his pottery.

We met and visited with several more potters before returning to the *minshuku* (bed and breakfast) where we would spend the night. The three of us expected to sleep in one room but found that the futons had been put down in two. One of the benefits of travel that we experienced in Japan is the identical nature of the sleeping arrangements: always on the floor with a warm down blanket and bean filled pillow. No worry about getting used to a new mattress or pillow as you move from place to place. The only variation we ever found was the thickness of the pillow and even then, not so big a change to prevent us from falling sleep.

A Japanese breakfast of soup, rice, cold fish, a salad, pickles, and tea was served in our room at 8:30. An hour later we were in a shop around the corner buying gifts to take home, while Robert had a long chat with the shopkeeper about the owner of the shop, a retired potter. The potter was more than eighty years old. We saw a small *sake* cup he had made when he was about twenty years old that sold for twenty or thirty yen then. Today it is 150,000 yen or about $1,200 at the current rate of exchange. We admired a small, exquisite incense burner that was priced at 500,000 yen—this amount for pottery from a man who was still living. The large bowls and vases were truly untouchable. Robert owns one of his *sake* cups and considers it a most important part of his collection.

Our next stop was the Nakamura workshop and kiln. The younger Mr. Nakamura, about forty-five years old, is a great friend of Robert's, and we were cordially invited into the workshop. The elder Mr. Nakamura, a seventy-seven-year-old, was at his wheel making water jars.

We wanted to purchase some dishes produced by the younger Nakamura. He left us for a moment and returned with six salad-size dishes. When we said we would take them, he gave them to his wife to wrap. Robert asked how much they would be and we were all taken aback when Mr. Nakamura said "Presento."

Robert firmly protested. Mr. Nakamura persisted saying, "they all have cracks and flaws and I wouldn't be able to sell them." A typical Japanese attitude of humility. The plates are gorgeous and any small flaw you might find adds to their earthiness.

We thanked him to the point that he was embarrassed and then left. Robert promised us that he would send them a bottle of sake when we returned home.

The rest of the day we saved for the Isezaki family.

Mr. Isezaki is quite famous at the age of fifty-six. Robert has visited him in Bizen many times, increasing his knowledge and his friendships with the potters and their families. Mrs. Isezaki is an environmentalist, as is Robert.

The Isezaki compound consists of four or five buildings set along a small river that flows through the town. The first building is an ancient, thatched roof farmhouse that has been restored and used as a gallery. The three rooms are open to a wooden porch where large plates, urns, and vases are dramatically displayed. We were served tea in one room surrounded by shelves of small "Isezaki" creations. Mrs. Isezaki told Robert how much she appreciated our coming, that it was fate and their good fortune to have the opportunity to meet Americans through their pottery.

When Mr. Isezaki appeared a few moments after we finished our tea, we were again greeted warmly. Mr. Isezaki is a tall, powerfully built man with a full head of blue-gray hair. His face had the shine of contentment and his eyes the sparkle of good humor. He, too, thought it was fate that brought us to his home.

We discussed our families; both of us have four sons. He asked what our sons do for a living and I told him. When I asked him the same question, he said they all work with him as potters. Mr. Isezaki's father had been a potter, and as each generation leaves this earth, the eldest son inherits the kiln, the homes, and the tradition continues. He also told us he writes Haiku. "As a matter of fact," he said, "eleven of my friends and I are going to walk through the town tomorrow, absorbing the season, and then we will return to this room to write poetry." He is an extremely talented human being.

We were served a splendid plate of *sushi* for lunch. Eating it from beautiful pottery makes it taste much better. I had to have one of his *sake* cups and asked Robert how much they would cost, fully expecting that I could not afford one. I was told not to worry, and Mr. Isezaki brought in a half a dozen for me to examine. I had difficulty deciding on one but finally did. It was the largest and fit my hand the best and had markings that appealed to my eye. I was amazed when Mrs. Isezaki told me it was 5000 yen. Later we found out that this was less than a quarter of the usual price for an Isezaki *sake* cup.

Following lunch Mrs. Isezaki suggested we ride into the countryside to a famous school site where the leaves were turning colors on the hillsides. The Shizutani School is the oldest free school in the world. It was built in 1666 by the feudal lord of the Bizen area and has been in use since. The roof tiles are all Bizen, made in kilns specially constructed on the school site. Ikeda Mitsumasa, the lord, believed that "Better public morality depends on the education of the common people." As true then as today.

The grounds are set on a grassy plain against a

hillside covered with leafy trees and evergreens. Our tour guide, Mrs. Isezaki, explained the significance of an imposing main lecture hall that stands at the far end of the entry onto the plain. "Once a day all the students would gather there before going to class. The entire student body could be seated for their daily lecture." The wooden floor of the main building still shines, even after all of these years.

We returned to the town, picked up our pottery, and said our good-byes to the Isezaki family. I told Mr. Isezaki that we would be most honored if he would visit us in America on his next trip. He looked at me and spoke slowly, forcefully and gently, all the while looking me square in the eyes. "I have never been out of Japan and probably never will leave my country. I don't even like to leave Bizen. Here I have everything any man needs, my family, my work, my home. What could I possibly find better away from here?" I was taken aback by this explanation of his life, and inspired by the simplicity and wholeness of his existence. I could find no response to a man who has found such a purity of purpose in his life.

Those experiences, and meeting Robert's friends, have given me much comfort. It had not been easy accepting Robert's decision to live in Japan. It is reassuring knowing that he has so much support from his surroundings. His decision is correct for him, no matter how difficult it is for Helene and me.

Before leaving Japan we spent an evening with the Takesues, Robert's employer. They took us to a unique restaurant called a *robatori*. The food—shell fish, huge mushrooms and fresh vegetables—was displayed on icy trays in full view of the customers sitting at a bar. After choosing your selection, the chef would cook it on an open fire, place your cooked serving on a long, wooden "spatula" and put it in front of you. The food was delicious.

It was there that Robert finally told us of his plans to marry Takako in the fall. "I've realized," he said, "that she is the person I want to share my life with.

"Before I got involved with Takako, I had known in my heart that I wanted to marry a Japanese woman," our son continued. "I know people say that cross-cultural marriages are difficult, but I don't feel it will be too much trouble. I think it will be just two people getting married, nothing unusual.

"The differences in culture, language, or religion don't have to be boundaries. Those differences are just a natural part of any marriage. Even in America, where the people have pretty much the same religion and the same language, the divorce rate is fifty per-cent. So, as I have thought it through, I don't feel we face something insurmountable. If we just have an open mind and learn from each other, we will get along very well."

We were not surprised at the news, we almost expected it. Takako had indicated this to me and Robert was of the age to be interested in women and marriage, and he had always been attracted to quiet girls. Helene knew that he would be attracted to the quietness of Japanese women. When Robert finished talking, Helene asked, "Do you love her?"

"Of course I love her, Mom," he replied. "Perhaps not in the American romantic way, but I love her for what she is and what she will be. She will make a good wife and a wonderful mother. I am as much interested in that as I am in having an old-fashioned love affair. Most of my friends in America who married their high school girl friends are divorced now. I just don't want that to happen to me."

We were pleased, dismayed, excited for them, and confused—at the same time. We had to consider the practical questions: Where would they live? Would they stay in Japan, or move to the States? What would Robert's grandparents think? We were so concerned about their reaction that we wondered if we should even tell them.

Then I started to become aware of my feelings. I had thought about the war these past few years, but not in this context. What would my reaction be? And, of course, we didn't know what to expect from Takako's parents. Would Robert be accepted into a Japanese family? They had not met Robert and, apparently, were unaware of his intentions. I turned to Yas and asked "Do you know Takako's family?"

"No, Jerry, I don't. But since I will be Robert's go-between, I will meet them soon. It will be my duty to tell Mr. Yamakawa about you and your family and vouch for Robert."

"Please, Yas, see if you can find out about his background, what he does, his war experience, what he thinks about Americans, if he will accept Robert into his family."

"I will do my best to get as much information as I can. As you know, we Japanese are quite reluctant to talk about ourselves. It may be difficult getting details, but I will try."

The next afternoon Helene asked Takako how long it took before she knew she and Robert wanted to get married?

She glanced quickly at Robert, then said, with a shy smile, "I knew from my first meeting with Robert that he and I would get married. The first person I told about my feelings towards him," Takako continued in her slow, careful English, "was my best friend, Kiyo. At first she could not hide her amazement that the man I chose to be my future husband was a foreigner. But, after meeting him in person, she thought he wasn't a bad person, and she encouraged our relationship. I also called my close friends who had moved away from Mishima and asked for their opinions. Most of them felt that it was acceptable as long as I really loved him.

"However, several friends cautioned me not to forget that many unfortunate Japanese girls had been deceived by foreigners. I never thought that Robert could do that to me, and I began to allow myself to love him.

"On my first day at Kiddy College, in the office, Robert approached me and started a conversation. I was fascinated by this good-looking, serious, young American."

Takako had been talking across the table to Helene and me, hardly looking at Robert. Now she raised her eyes to him and smiled.

"Before I knew what was happening," she said, "I had agreed to have lunch with him. I almost forgot to ask him his name! That lunch was the first of many.

Very naturally we seemed to spend most of our spare time together. There was so much we had to learn from each other, and so much to learn about each other. Almost without realizing it, we drew closer and closer. I soon realized that Robert was as serious about me as I was about him from the first day that we met."

"Have you said anything to your parents yet?" Helene asked.

Takako answered, "No" and looked down. We realized then that it was going to be a problem for her. And it was.

Later Robert told us that the night she gave our gift of the bottle of brandy to her father, her mother's immediate response to Takako was, "I know you are interested in a *gaijin* from the phone calls and the pictures in your room. I want you to know that you can marry any Japanese man that you choose, but you will not bring a foreigner, especially one who was your father's enemy, into our family."

For centuries the Japanese had kept their society "pure" by making sure that no foreigners were allowed to become citizens. They also arranged marriages based on social status, education, and occupation. Many occupations are looked upon with disdain—grave diggers, leather tanners, and the Ainu, a Japanese sect—are not often invited into marriage, except within their own professions. For Hatsue, Takako's mother to say "you can marry any Japanese man you choose," she was referring to these so called "low caste" persons. This admission by Mrs. Yamakawa was an indication of the depth of their feelings about *gaijins* in general and Americans in particular.

It was a shock to Takako to hear this from her mother, the person she thought understood her most. She had expected her mother would be sympathetic because she had encountered serious opposition herself from the Yamakawa family when their son Taro wanted to marry her. Being *samurai*, his family objected to Taro marrying a woman who was of lower status.

CHAPTER
NINE

_____

Reflections

WE LEFT MISHIMA station for Narita Airport the next afternoon. Shortly after we boarded the Singapore Airlines 747 for the trip home, an announcement came over the loudspeaker, "Our flight to Los Angeles will take eight hours and ten minutes. We will arrive ahead of schedule at 11:45 A.M."

I looked at Helene and said, "that is only twenty minutes more than some of my missions." We were seated in wide, business class seats with foot rests that reclined to a comfortable sleeping position. I couldn't imagine sitting the entire flight to Los Angeles without getting out of my seat, having two meals, and taking a nap or two. And yet, that is how long our missions to Japan were. We sat on a bumpy survival kit and parachute, hands on the controls, no food, no relief for seven and a half hours.

"I don't know how you did it, Jer. You can't sit for ten minutes now without getting up for a walk." After a few minutes of reflection, Helene asked, "Are you upset about Robert?"

"Somewhat bothered, a little confused and apprehensive. I felt so comfortable in Japan. Every trip I see more that I like, more beauty, serenity. Maybe it's my imagination, but I think the older women never seem to look directly at me. And when they do, I wonder what they might be thinking. When I look at Fuji I see it through the rings of my gun sight, anti-aircraft fire bursting in the background. I just can't shake the war and what I felt then."

During the long flight I reflected on my apprehension about the impending marriage. There were, after all, religious, racial, and cultural differences that had to be faced. And then there was the war.

I was developing an appreciation for the culture of Japan and had cultivated friendships with several Japanese people. My heart was touched more than once by the people I had met, the children, Mr. Matsuda. That was one thing. But accepting them into my family was something else.

If Robert was going to marry a Japanese girl, I wanted to go beyond accepting the Japanese people. I needed to be able to embrace them. If they were to be part of our family, that meant I would have to love them. I wondered if I could.

I have never felt a closeness with organized religion. Although I insisted that my children be exposed to Judaism when they were young, it did not bother me that they were not observant when they were older. I wasn't, so why should they be? Since Helene and I had been practicing Transcendental Meditation, we have found great satisfaction in our meditations. Through this simple technique, we have become closer to our inner selves and, strangely, much more aware of a higher self. On the high holy days of our religion, we often walked the beach in what we referred to as "the synagogue of the open sky." Both of us had felt this closeness with nature in Japan. Shintoism, one of the major religions of Japan, is truly the worship of the natural world. I felt the religious differences between our families would not be difficult to overcome.

Culturally, I feel the Jews and the Japanese are very close. Family, education, respect for elders and tradition was how I was raised. From what I had seen in Japan, those traits are ingrained in the Japanese from birth. And regarding the difference in race, if I were true to my belief that we are all one and the same, that all humans live in one of nature's subdivisions, then race could not be an issue. But was it? The war with Japan presented a problem that extended beyond me. How would my parents feel if I had been killed and my sister brought home a Japanese man? How would my buddies feel? Would this marriage in some way negate what they fought and died for? Could I put these questions to rest once and for all?

I sensed the emotional reasons Takako's father might object to this marriage. Not only was Robert a caucasian, but he was the son of the enemy of his youth! There was no doubt, he, too, would face these unsettling questions.

After returning home to San Diego, I couldn't put my mind on anything. I tried to work, but time and time again a restlessness overtook me, and my mind filled with memories. Late one night, when Helene was asleep and the house was quiet, I sat down on the couch and opened my scrapbook.

My mother had started the scrapbook the day I went into the service, and she presented it to me when the war was over. Together we added pages of pictures, my citations, and other items that I had brought from Iwo. From time to time, when Helene and I moved or cleaned out a closet, I glanced at the scrapbook. Now, prompted by my youngest son, I sat down with the book and my memories to think about the war and my buddies.

I began to relive the war.

There was a photograph of me in my first uniform as a young recruit. The memories began flooding in, and I gave in to them. I had a vague fear that I might remember things perhaps best forgotten. But then again, maybe forgetting them had not been good for me.

As I started turning the pages, I thought, half-heartedly, that the picture on the first page should have been of me as a child building model airplanes, or poring over aviation magazines. From the time I was six, I loved planes and had a yearning to fly. I collected *Wings* magazines and knew all the flyers from World War I as well as the planes they flew. My friend Frank Turbett and I bought model airplane kits by pooling our "Greenies" and "Brownies"—the coupons we earned selling *Collier's* and *Liberty* magazines in our neighborhood. Our favorites were Spads and Fokkers, fighter planes from World War I. Frank was eleven and lived on the third floor of our house. He became an aeronautical engineer and helped build the airplanes that I flew.

Once, we had enough coupons to get a large flying model. We worked on this model on my dining room table until my mother discovered the deep razor blade cuts in the table's surface. We flew the plane from Frank's attic window and watched it crash on its first flight when it ran out of power. But the magic of building planes and flying them never left me.

When I read *Alone*, Charles Lindbergh's account of his historic solo flight in 1927, Lindy became my all-time hero. I flew with him across the Atlantic to a cheering welcome. During the war, quietly and without fanfare, Lindbergh flew most of our fighters on long, grueling, test missions. Those missions established the engine settings that allowed us to fly our long-range missions. Then in 1940, the war created new flying heroes. The battle for Britain against the mighty German forces was won by Spitfire and Hurricane pilots. Praising them, Churchill spoke of "the gratitude of so many to so few." I dreamed I was one of them.

But there were no pictures of me sitting at the table building model airplanes; the first snapshot was of an eighteen-year-old with his head shaved, wearing a new uniform and smiling.

I had reported for basic training at Fort Dix in my home state of New Jersey. Despite grueling exercises, endless drilling, and lectures from sharp-tongued sergeants, the six weeks passed quickly. Several more weeks were spent at Mitchell Field, on Long Island, New York while we waited to be assigned to a class.

At Mitchell Field I was assigned to the kitchen as an assistant cook. We were on duty for three meals and then had six meals off. This meant that after every working shift, I had two days of free time. On one of those free days, a beautiful spring afternoon, I was walking around on the flight line and noticed a young captain checking out one of the small military planes. I walked over, saluted, and asked him, "Are you flying somewhere today?"

"Yes."

"Do you have room for a passenger?"

"I don't know. I'm flying a bunch of brass down to Washington, D.C. But hang around; if there's an empty seat, I'll take you with me."

I waited, and in a short while six lieutenant colonels arrived and got on board. It was an eight-passenger Cessna, so there was room, although I didn't know if I'd be invited to join them. As soon as everyone was on board the pilot said, "Okay, Cadet, climb in!"

We flew the colonels down to Andrews Air Force Base, and on the way back to Mitchell Field, I sat in the co-pilot's seat and handled the controls. For me it was the realization of a long dream to be at the controls of an airplane, and this on my first flight in a military airplane. I didn't have a photograph of it, but it is still completely vivid in my mind. I had waited many years for that first flight.

In October we were sent to Nashville for classification testing. What we did there would determine our future assignment in the Air Corps. We were subjected to weeks of physical, psychological, and intellectual testing. At the end of six weeks, the results were posted. I was given the choice of bombardier, navigator, or pilot. Without hesitation I chose pilot. Flying as a navigator or a bombardier in a large, slow airplane was not to my liking. I wanted to have the freedom that came with flying a fighter plane.

In November of 1942, our class was assigned to Santa Ana, California for Pre-Flight School. We spent fourteen days crossing the country. As we started across Texas, one of the cadets, Joe Webb, locked all of the doors to the toilets on the train, "so no damn Yankee craps on Texas!"

In Santa Ana we lived in barracks, sixty to a floor, two floors to a building. I was in the class of 43H. Those of us who completed the training would graduate in August of 1943 as pilots.

The following months were filled with exhilaration and wonder. I loved the discipline and camaraderie. Reveille and roll call were at five-thirty in the morning and lights out at ten in the evening. Every minute in between was filled with ground school classes in navigation, radio, Morse code, and aerodynamics. There was physical training for strength and endurance, and parade ground drilling for discipline.

On Saturdays we had dress review in full uniform, marching squadron by squadron across the parade ground. The music stirred my heart. To see the American flag held high then dipped in salute gave me a great feeling of pride in my country and in myself for being a part of the military. Each of us wanted our squadron to be the best, so we could carry the banner and lead the parade the following week.

The war was still something distant, hardly real at all.

There were pictures of Doris Rosen. I met her on my first weekend leave, when I was a cadet in Santa Ana in early 1943. I was given her phone number by a friend in New Jersey and spent four hours hitchhiking to her home in Los Angeles. I still remember the absolute shock of shyness that overcame me when I saw her. She was slightly taller than I and much, much prettier than any girl I had ever known. She was beautiful, tall and slim with long legs and long, dark hair. I fell in love at first sight.

I was only eighteen, shy with girls, and could not believe my good fortune. At first I thought it was my uniform that attracted her, as her beauty had impressed me. In a short time I thought of her as "my girl." When not busy with activities or studying, my mind was filled with Doris. I called her as often as I could and even wrote to her from Santa Ana. I saw her every weekend until I left for further training at Thunderbird Army Air Base in Phoenix.

When we were assigned airplanes, I named mine the "Dorrie R," and kept Doris's picture on the instrument panel. Although we only saw each other eight or ten times throughout the war, I looked forward to seeing her again. She must have felt the same, as she sent me hundreds of letters. My memories of Doris and those letters helped bring me home alive.

During training, mail call came to be the most important event of our day, second only to "chow call." Food nourished our bodies, letters from home nourished our morale. In a combat zone, in danger of not surviving, mail from home was our only link with the reality of the outside world.

The next photo was of me sitting in the cockpit of a Stearman biplane. I made my first solo flight in that plane.

Flight training began in earnest in February at Thunderbird Field. I had always admired the Spad pilots in war movies when they leaned out the side and yelled, "Contact." Now I was leaning out the side of this open cockpit biplane and yelling, "Clear, contact," and watching the propeller spin and the engine cough, then start.

On Washington's Birthday, 1943, five days after we started flying, I was the first in my class to solo. During training I had sat in the rear seat, communicating with the instructor through a speaking tube. His head became a reference point I could use to line up for maneuvers. When the instructor got out of the plane and told me to take it up alone, reality hit me and I had doubts. Can I do it? Not only was one of my major frames of reference gone, there was no comforting knowledge that no matter what I might do, he was there to help out!

Everything looked and felt different as I taxied out to the end of the runway and waited for the green light from the tower. When it came I advanced the throttle slowly, and in a moment, it seemed, I was in the air alone.

I climbed to three thousand feet, did some stalls, some steep turns, gaining confidence with every minute. Getting up was easy, I thought, but landing in the crosswind could be more difficult. The Stearman has a lot of wing surface and a narrow landing gear, making it very sensitive to the wind. Desert winds have a nasty habit of changing rapidly, and I wanted to land without incident. Occasionally the wind would be so strong that we had to land with full throttle and then be held down by someone on the wing tips as we taxied.

After thirty minutes I headed back to the field, entered the pattern and started my descent. The wind whistling through the struts sounded the same as when the instructor was in the plane. I surprised myself by making a good landing. It all felt quite natural, as if I had been doing it for a long time. I was proud of myself. Then I taxied to the flight line where I was congratulated by my classmates and the instructor. By tradition I had everyone sign a dollar bill. The signed bill was called, for some reason, a "short snorter." I carried it with me for luck throughout the war.

Pilot training was divided into three sections: Primary, Basic, and Advanced. Goals had to be met at each section or you were "washed out" of training. By the time we graduated, about half of the class was gone. Each stage presented challenges that were unique. At Primary, which I had just completed, the challenge was learning to fly.

In April we were sent to Maranna Army Air Base in Tucson, Arizona to begin Basic Flight School. At Basic, the aircraft engine was larger, and the plane was more sophisticated. In addition, we were taught the disciplines we would need to survive combat. Good precision flying in formation was critical, along with aerobatics, navigation, and radio procedures. When we were not in ground school, we studied mechanics.

Life in the desert was hectic and focused. Each day was more exciting than the previous one as we pushed ourselves to get more out of the planes. We performed aerobatics, did touch and go landings, and flew in close formation. I loved the smell of the planes, the noise on the flight line, and of course, the flying. My dreams were coming true.

At Luke Field in Phoenix, we learned about war. We were taught what a fighter plane was built for. We made simulated strafing runs and flew night missions, and then, in July, we went to gunnery school at Gila Bend, Arizona.

When not flying, we studied enemy aircraft silhouettes and performance charts. Since we did not know which theater of operations we would be assigned to, we had to learn all the German, Italian, and Japanese planes. Our final exams would include flying and gunnery proficiency tests, as well as high-speed airplane identification. Failing any part meant transfer to bombers. Or worse yet, to transports!

But after passing all of my flight and ground school tests, I failed the eye test again. When the doctor told me he was going to recommend that I be put in transports, I said, "There's no way that I'm going to fly transports. I'm a fighter pilot. I'm going to fly a fighter."

I had always been a loner. In a fighter, a man is alone. You have no co-pilot, no gunner; you're on your own. That's what I wanted.

When America entered the war, I made up my

mind to find the toughest job and become as good or better at it than anyone else. For me, that meant becoming a fighter pilot. Even though I was a Jew, I only wanted to fight against the "Japs." They were the ones who attacked my country.

I also knew that my number wasn't up. I was certain that nothing was going to happen to me in the war, but I didn't want to be in somebody else's airplane when his number was up!

The doctor said that the only person who could recommend me for flying fighters, since my eyesight wasn't up to standard, was the Commanding Officer of the base.

I said, "How do I get to see him?"

"I'd have to get permission from the Flight Surgeon."

"Would you do it for me?"

He said yes, and he did. Soon the call came from a staff sergeant to report to the Colonel's office. I walked into the office and saluted. The Colonel was tall and imposing, dressed in his summer uniform with his Colonel's eagle on his shoulder and wings on his chest. I was frightened. Not just because I was an Aviation Cadet and he was a full Colonel, but he had the power to let me fly fighters or to ship me out and I did not want to ship out.

"What can I do for you, Cadet Yellin?"

"Sir, I only want to fly fighters. They want to assign me to transports because I have 20/30 vision. But I can see and fly as well as anyone in my class and my records will prove it."

He looked at me. I was grim, standing at rigid

attention, my heart pounding. After what seemed an age he said, "Anyone with the guts to come see me on a matter such as this, is the kind of man we want flying fighters. You will fly fighters. I will see to it that you do. Dismissed."

That was all; but when I walked out, I was elated. I couldn't believe it! I would get my hours in the Curtiss P-40 and graduate with my class.

The P-40 was a war plane, not a trainer. There was room only for a pilot. Up until now, we always had an instructor with us when we checked out in a new plane. Now, I was on my own from the first flight. I had not felt self-doubt or fear until that moment. It wasn't the fear of being killed, or even of getting hurt. It was the fear of failing, of getting this far and no further. But then there was the excitement of actually starting up this top-of-the-line combat plane and taking off, alone. It was the culmination of all my dreams of what flying could be. And there I was, ready to switch on the mags and do it!

The feel of the leather seat, the panel full of instruments, the smell of the high-octane aviation fuel, was awesome. The engine had a distinctive, fast putt-putt sound when taxiing, and a smooth, high-pitched whine in the air.

From inside the cockpit with the canopy closed, the sound was muffled. I felt the power of the engine as I taxied to the end of the runway. I tentatively advanced the throttle. The plane leapt forward, my head was thrown back, and the torque nearly pulled me off the runway! Before I knew it, I was at 4,000 feet, at 8,000 feet before I got the gear up! I pointed the long nose at a cloud in the sky, eased back on the stick and climbed. At 15,000 feet I leveled off, cleared below and started a dive to get enough speed to do a loop. My confidence grew with every maneuver, slow role, Immelman, lazy eights. At the end of an hour, I was confident that I could fly as well as anyone.

Strangely, I remembered the day I got my driver's license and drove a car alone for the first time. How careful I was when I passed a parked car, pulling far away. Then as time went by, it became a game to see how close I could drive to a parked car. The same thing happened to me in the first fifty hours of flying a fighter.

At one time I was a pretty good golfer, and I know that there are certain moments in the sport when you are one with the ball, and one with the club. It doesn't happen all the time, but there are moments when everything is in synch, and you're just not even there.

That's the way I felt about flying, once I had mastered the mechanics and didn't have to think about what I was doing or had to do next. There was an inanimate object called "an airplane," but when I got in it, I became the heart and the pulse, and I made that inanimate object alive.

Flying became a religious experience. I never felt that "I" was flying an "airplane." The airplane was not something separate from me. The airplane was me, it was responding to me, it was the same as me.

As a wing man, I never knew whether I was upside down or in a steep turn. I just knew I was tucked in tight on the wing of my leader in coordination and harmony with my airplane and his.

Once I got in the air, everything else in my life was gone. I felt the sky, and my boundaries expanded. That detachment from the earth was a tremendous freedom.

All through training, I couldn't wait to get up in the morning to fly. And it was the same during the war. Forget about the danger; there was never a thought of it. Forget about the hazards of war, forget about killing; I didn't even think about that. All I wanted was to fly that airplane.

In fact, the whole experience of the war became something like that for me. I had a sense of purpose, of mission, that gave my life meaning. I felt that our presence in the war was right and just, that we had been attacked and were entirely right to fight back and kill the people who had attacked us. That sense of purpose motivated my every waking moment until the war ended—then it left me.

The excitement, the dedication, the military discipline, the war was a hard act to follow. Any work I did as a civilian was more out of necessity than passion.

In June, I was sent to Luke Field, near Phoenix for the Advanced phase of single-engine fighter training. Those of us who didn't wash out would graduate in August. During the last weeks of training, we flew P-40s. I posed in front of one with four friends from Santa Ana—Ruby, Sherren, Roseberry, and Patterson—our arms around each other's shoulders. Five, happy, cocky, young guys with dreams for the future.

To celebrate our impending graduation and the receipt of our airman wings, we did what every other class before us had done—we buzzed the Grand Canyon, flying below the rim and risking being caught and washed out. At the graduation ceremony we were given our wings and second lieutenant bars for our uniforms. Gold bars on my collar and silver wings on my chest. I felt proud.

The enlisted men lined up to salute us, and each of them collected a dollar for the first salute of a new officer.

When I saw the picture on the next page of the scrapbook, I laughed out loud. I was standing with my arm around Bonita Granville, the actress.

There was nothing that young women found more glamorous during the war than a pilot. All of us were trim and fit, looked good in our officer's uniform and were available. Some might even have thought that I was handsome.

After I graduated from flying school, I was sent to Oakland, California for a few days, awaiting transportation to Hawaii. I was the only flying officer on the small base. While there, I was asked to escort a beautiful Hollywood starlet appearing in one of the USO shows near San Francisco. The show starred George Jessel, John Bowles, and Bonita Granville.

After the show, Bonita and I went to the Mark Hopkins Hotel for lunch. We chatted a while about the show, about San Francisco, about our backgrounds. Then she got a serious look on her face, and, eyeing my pilot wings, she said, "Everyone in

Hollywood has an airplane named for her; Betty Grable has a bomber named after her. You know, Lieutenant, I would do anything—and I mean anything—to have an airplane named after me."

There I was in the hotel, with a beautiful actress leaning halfway across the table to say this to me, and the entire afternoon free. So what did I say?

"Gee, I'm sorry Miss Granville, but I've already named my airplane after someone."

Today when I tell that story, even my wife says, "You lost an opportunity that many would have accepted on the spot." I have to agree that today, I might say something different.

CHAPTER
TEN

---

*The 78th Fighter
Squadron*

TEN DAYS AFTER graduation, I sailed under the Golden Gate Bridge on a merchant marine freighter. We were loaded with empty gasoline drums and worried about submarines until we arrived in Hawaii a few days later. I reported to the 78th Fighter Squadron in Haliewa, on Oahu. My classmates, Sherren, Roseberry, and Ruby, arrived shortly afterwards. We were told that we would receive fifty hours of training before being shipped out to a combat zone. It was October 1943, and the Pacific offensive was beginning at Makin and Tarawa, atolls in the Marshall Islands.

I was assigned to the wing of Vic Mollan, in Jim Tapp's flight. Every day we flew our P-40s on simulated combat missions, one day dive-bombing targets in the sea, other days strafing, always flying in formation. We had been trained as pilots in the States, but now we honed our skills and become combat pilots.

We flew hard in training, under conditions that were as close as possible to those we would face in actual battle. We flew simulated air-to-air missions against other Air Corps squadrons as well as against the Navy. The rivalry between the services was intense, and we enjoyed dog-fighting against the Marines in their F4U Corsairs and the Navy in their F6F Hellcats.

On one individual aerial mission against Vic Mollan, I tried too hard to get on his tail and entered into a high-speed spin. I spun down through the clouds and came out of the spin heading through the Pali, a mountain pass. Luckily, I was going in the right direction, or I would have been plastered against the side of the mountain.

The basic formation of a flight was four planes split into two pairs called elements. The first pair consisted of the flight leader and his wing man; the second, the element leader and his wing man.

When the flight leader wiggled the tail of his plane, the element leader and his wing man would slide off, taking a position several hundred yards away. Then, when the flight leader turned toward his element, they would each have an opportunity to scan the sky to the rear of the flight and take up opposite positions as the planes crisscrossed the sky. This maneuver, known as "mutual support," allowed the pilots to look out for one another.

On one such mission in December 1943, in Mokuleia, Howard Edmonson collided with our Squadron Commander, Major Bill Southerland. Southerland was killed. Edmonson bailed out and survived—but only for a few months.

When I joined the 78th, Edmonson was a class or two ahead of our group. He was several years older than me, a married man, more experienced in the world. At twenty-three or twenty-four, he seemed to belong to another generation. Howard became pretty close to my cadet buddies, Roseberry, Ruby, and Sherren, because all four of them were from Iowa.

Although Howard and I never did become close friends, we were linked by a common trait that set us apart from most others—we didn't drink. Once a month, every officer received a fifth of whiskey as part of our rations. Because I wasn't a drinker, I either gave it away or traded it for something else.

Not being a drinker left me out of many of the social activities in the service. I was never really comfortable in situations that required alcohol as the catalyst for conversation and camaraderie. This set me apart from my squadron mates and perhaps kept me from getting close to many of them.

For his own reasons, Howard was similar. He was a religious, serious, young man, a Bible-toting Christian, what we called an "early-to-bedder, do-gooder" kind of guy. Never in my civilian life had I met anybody with that kind of religious fervor.

Shortly after I joined the squadron in Hawaii, Howard received a letter with disturbing news from one of his friends in the States. What that news was, we never found out, but he started to drink. He went completely the other way. I remember Sherren, Ruby, and Roseberry all trying to console him and get him straightened out, but nothing eased his torment.

On that flight in December 1943, Howard had the midair collision that killed Major Southerland. Several months later, in June 1944, flying a P-47, he slammed into the side of a mountain and died in a fiery crash.

Perhaps he didn't kill himself intentionally, but he flew when he was not supposed to fly, under conditions in which he knew he shouldn't fly. He had been drinking the night before. Alcohol and flying don't mix.

During our training in a ground pressure tank that simulated high altitudes, the trainer asked for a volunteer to take his mask off so we could see the effect of lack of oxygen, and why it was important to wear an oxygen mask when flying over 10,000 feet. When you fly to higher altitudes, you develop a shortage of oxygen in your blood, a condition known as anoxia. Alcohol does the same thing: it absorbs the oxygen, and that's what gives you the dizzy feeling.

Bob Ruby took his mask off at "10,000 feet," and the instructor said, "Okay, write your name." He wrote "Robert C. Ruby." But as pressure took us up a little higher, he wrote "Robert C. Robert," then "Ruby Ruby Ruby." As we kept getting higher, he kept getting more and more drunk, until his fingers started turning blue and then his oxygen mask was replaced.

Edmonson was the first soldier I knew who was killed. His death was the first hint—and it was just a hint, no more than that—of the reality of war. We were boys, eighteen, nineteen years old, on an adventure, flying expensive airplanes, seeing the world. We had no idea what war was like.

Thinking about this, I put the scrapbook down and went to the kitchen, heated up some water, and made myself a cup of coffee. The night was quiet, but not my heart. I walked around the living room holding the cup in my hand for awhile, then sat down again and turned the page.

The picture I saw was one that had always made me proud. It was me, standing next to my first plane, the Dorrie R, with my name painted on its side.

Our fifty hours of combat training passed quickly, and I was promoted to First Lieutenant and given my first plane. Hating the Japanese as I did, I was eager to move into a combat squadron. I wanted to be in the war and at them . . . but for the present I had to remain in Hawaii with the 78th Fighter Squadron, flying Island Defense and training other pilots in combat maneuvers.

Some of the pilots of 78th had been based at Wheeler Field on the day Pearl Harbor was attacked and had suffered the first casualties in World War II. On August 15, 1945, the last day of the war, I was in the air with the 78th over Japan. We lost one pilot. He may have been the last casualty of the war.

All of us in the squadron felt that the 78th was the best outfit in the military. And it wasn't just a feeling. We had a reputation in the service for being the best fliers, and our combat records attested to that. Jim Tapp, our squadron leader, shot down four airplanes the first time he was in combat. Tapp was without question the best pilot in the Air Force, at least in the Pacific.

Todd Moore—we called him "Baby" Moore, but not to his face—shot down eighteen Japanese airplanes. At twenty-one years of age, the Air Force transferred him from the 78th and made him the squadron leader of the 45th. In fact, the 78th produced many of the leaders for the other fighter squadrons.

When President Roosevelt arrived in Hawaii on a destroyer in 1944 to meet with General MacArthur, headquarters called the 78th to put on an air show. They told Jim Tapp, "Pick a wing man and go up and do an hour show for the President."

Jim chose me. "Yellin," he said, "let's go. Get on my wing and don't get off. If you get off, you'll be sorry you ever flew."

We were flying from a golf course at Schofield Barracks in Hawaii. Jim and I took off in formation, and I never left his wing. We buzzed the destroyer, we did lazy eights, rolls, and loops; anything you could do in a fighter plane, we did—in perfect formation. We put on a fantastic show for President Roosevelt.

The members of the 78th shared a camaraderie and a sense of purpose that continues to link us together, even fifty years after the war.

One of the customs that set us apart was our commander's insistence that rank be left at the door of the Officers' Club. This was highly unusual in the military, which is ruled by a virtual caste system based on rank. Our rule was that no officer could enter while wearing signs of his rank. "Gook shirts"—colorful Hawaiian prints—were the only uniform permitted. This gave us all a chance, seldom available otherwise, to fraternize with higher ranking officers on a common level.

Most evenings were spent in our Officers' Club. Whatever romantic images that term may conjure up, the reality was a shack located in the woods of Haliewa. For entertainment, we didn't have dance bands and pretty girls; we had card games and conversation and, for some, drinking.

Jack Patterson, one of the cadets from Luke Field, was from Hawaii. Jack led us on several weekend escapades into Waikiki. But even on our time off, we carried gas masks and wore our sidearm.

On March 10, 1944, we were on a gunnery mission fifty miles off Kahuka Point. I was at 12,000 feet making an overhead pass at a tow target when my engine went out of control. It raced past the "red line" to 5,000 rpm in a split second and then froze. I had no choice but to bail out. At 8,000 feet I trimmed the nose down, cleared my seat belt and shoulder harness, rolled back the canopy and turned the plane upside-down. I popped the stick and was sucked out of the aircraft at 230 mph. The rip cord came free in my hand when I grabbed it. I thought the chute had failed!

It hadn't. I came to a sudden, abrupt, and painful stop in midair. When I looked up at the canopy I was hanging from, it looked about the size of a dime.

All parachutes used in over-water flights were equipped with life rafts. These were packed into the seat of the chute and the cover had to be released before you reached the water. I pushed out of the chute at what I thought was five or ten feet above the waves. It turned out to be more like twenty or thirty! The impact flipped me over backwards, breaking the cord on my Mae West, my life preserver. When I inflated it, my head was pushed backwards, into the water, and I had to struggle to keep from drowning.

I eventually got the life raft out safely, climbed into it, and then spent nine hours bobbing about in the ocean watching out for sharks, although there was nothing much I could have done if any had appeared. Finally, a crash boat from Honolulu reached me. Pilots from my squadron had kept me in sight all along and directed the rescue ship. I didn't get back to the base until two in the morning.

Exhausted, I went right to sleep. Four hours later, I was awakened and told to fly a plane back over the ocean. I had difficulty starting the engine. The crew chief climbed on the wing, leaned into the cockpit and turned on the mag switch. When it did start I smelled an unusually strong odor of gas. I was frightened and didn't want to fly but I was ordered to, so I did. The flight cured me of any fear that might have developed if I had been given time to think about what had happened.

When I bailed out, I did everything automatically. There had been no training for it, only discussions of what to do under every conceivable circumstance. Few men who bailed out of fighters actually survived. Some hit the tail of the plane when they left the cockpit. Others, we assume, were hit on the side of their heads by the shroud lines and knocked unconscious. Survivors of bailouts described both of these events.

A year after I bailed out, I told a group of new pilots about my experience. One of the men, Walt Kreinman, had his plane shot up on a mission over Tokyo. Reacting as I had instructed him, he managed to get out safely from his burning P-51 Mustang at a very low altitude. No one saw him bail out and he was reported killed in action. However, he was picked up by a submarine a few hours later and taken back to Guam.

Many years later, on a Sunday afternoon, my telephone rang and I was asked, "Is this Jerry Yellin?" When I replied, "It is," the tone on the other end of the phone became quite excited. It was Walt Kreinman calling. He told me he had been asking my whereabouts for years and had finally gotten my telephone number at the first 78th reunion he attended the previous week. He was calling to thank me for giving him a wife, children, grandchildren, and forty-three years of living. I didn't know what he was talking about. He explained that when he was hit on a mission over Tokyo, he had about three seconds to get out of his plane before it exploded. If it hadn't been for me telling him to practice bailing out in his mind until he could do it without thinking, he would not have lived. He just wanted me to know how grateful he and his family were to me. I was touched by his gratitude.

A few months after my bail-out, I traded my Curtis P-40K Kitty Hawk for a Republic P-47D Thunderbolt. A big plane, nearly twice the weight of a P-40. It was dubbed "the Jug." Most of the P-47s flew well, but a few still had tools rattling around inside the fuselage, left by some factory worker. From a performance standpoint, the P-47 far exceeded the P-40. It was faster, could climb quicker, had better range and altitude, and greater firepower. One of its vices was a tendency to go into a flat spin, which was invariably fatal.

One time, in a test dive in a Jug, I hit 580 mph. I felt the vibrations caused by compressed air in front of the wings. I knew that if I didn't react immediately, the nose of the plane would start to tuck under and I wouldn't be able to pull out. I fired the guns, gave it full throttle, and hit the water injection to get the nose up. I had started into the dive at 40,000 feet and managed to pull out at 10,000 feet. It was a close call.

A few days after getting our Jugs, I heard Ed Green over the radio shouting, "Mayday! Mayday! I'm in a flat spin and can't get out!"

I heard Merrill, his classmate and buddy, pleading, "Jump, Ed! Jump!" Then there was silence. We searched the area for days looking for oil slicks. We found none and finally abandoned the search.

Ed was the first of my close friends to be killed. We were ballplayers together on our squadron softball team. He played first base and I played second. Losing him was a shock. He was a team leader, always giving encouragement to the ball club no matter what the score. And he was usually the first to take a new pilot under his wing and to teach him the ropes. At least that is what he did for me. And now, he was gone, not transferred, but gone forever.

A memorial service was held, then we continued with our scheduled training. That's how it was in war time.

Shortly after Ed's death we received our first P-51D-20-NA North American Mustang, and by year's end there were only a few P-47s left.

The P-51D looked and felt like a fighter should, small (8000 pounds empty) with beautiful lines. It responded to the controls instantly and, with a new, high speed wing, it was a match in maneuverability for the Zero, a Japanese fighter plane. The Mustang, with a 1650hp Packard-built Rolls Royce Merlin engine, was the fastest piston plane of its time. It could sustain 400 mph in straight and level flight. Critical to the long range mission, it held 269 gallons of fuel internally and two 100 gallon external wing tanks. Though not nearly as rugged as the Jug, it was described "like a gazelle compared to a water buffalo." It handled differently from the 47 and we had a lot to learn. It was the airplane that we would fly in against the Japanese.

In December 1944, we finally headed into combat. Not until we had put to sea did we learn of our actual destination: Iwo Jima.

On the fifteen-day boat trip to Guam, we lived luxuriously, by Army standards. We slept on linen sheets, ate with real silver, dined on roasts, steaks, and turkey every night, watched movies and played volleyball in a huge elevator. When we arrived at Guam in mid-January 1945, we off-loaded the Mustangs and flew from there to Saipan, to await our part in the invasion and capture of Iwo Jima.

Iwo Jima is an eight square mile volcanic island, eight hundred miles south of mainland Japan. From the air it looks like a giant manta ray sleeping in the ocean. A line drawn on a map from Guam to Tokyo would almost bisect Iwo. General "Hap" Arnold,

Commander-in-Chief of the Army Air Corps, decided
early in the war that strategic bombing of Japan would
require the capture of Iwo.

He was right. In American hands, Iwo served
three important purposes. It was used as a jumping-off
place for fighters to escort the B-29 bombers; it eliminated the early sighting of the B-29s by the Japanese
and the warning of raids on Japan; and it provided an
emergency landing area for crippled bombers returning from the mainland. All of the land-based fighter
missions over Japan would originate on Iwo. By the
time the war ended, 2,400 crippled B-29s had also
landed there, saving the lives of 27,000 American airmen.

But first Iwo had to be taken. The Marines had
begun the invasion on February 19, 1945. By early
March they had captured half of the island. The
Japanese remained dug in on the northern half of Iwo.
It would be months before the entire island was cap-
tured. By the time the island was secure several
months later, 26,000 men had been killed: 20,000
Japanese and 6,000 Americans.

On March 7 I flew from Saipan to Iwo Jima with
the Fifteenth Fighter group. I was in the heart of the
war for the first time since enlisting. The island had
been ravaged by bombs and heavy shells; fires were
burning; smoke was thick in the air. On the side of the
runway, piles of Japanese bodies were barely covered
by mounds of earth.

The air was filled with the sickening, heavy,
unbearable smell of death. It was overwhelming. I
have lived with that smell every day of my life since

then. You never get rid of it. It's like having cigarette smoke embedded in a wool jacket; you put the jacket on, and you smell it. The smell of death rarely leaves me.

That day, we dug foxholes, ate our K rations, and crawled into the ground as soon as it got dark. The sound of machine guns and mortars echoed throughout the night.

The next morning we flew our first mission. Immediately after take off, we were strafing enemy troops. It became our daily routine to strafe for the Marines on Iwo, and then fly to nearby Chichi Jima. We carried two 50-pound bombs to dive bomb and strafe the harbor and airfield there. There was always antiaircraft flak, and we sustained damage and some losses.

Despite the danger, I was glad to finally be fighting the Japanese.

I have many memories of Iwo that were not connected to the fighting.

One of the first officers I spoke to when we arrived on Iwo was Doc Lewis, our flight surgeon. Doc had a great sense of humor but was terribly bored with life as "family" doctor for our squadron. While we were in Hawaii, he used to stand at the end of the flight line and kid us, saying things like, "I wish I had a good accident so I could see some blood and broken bones. I'm tired of treating sore throats, and ingrown toenails, and athlete's foot. . . Come on you guys, have a good accident!" He was only kidding, of course. We were his boys and he suffered terribly when one of us was hurt or lost.

Before we left Hawaii, Doc was assigned to a hospital ship for the invasion of Iwo Jima. When we landed on Iwo and saw him again, his playfulness was gone. He looked older, tired, something was different about Doc from that day forward. Without going into detail, he told us he had seen all he needed of the terrible bloodshed, the dead and wounded Marines, the suffering. When he greeted us, he said, "I take it all back. I wish I could go back to treating sore throats."

We were never far from the front on Iwo. The Marines were under pressure at all times. Their gains were made in yards, one at a time. Several weeks after we landed, we had a respite from the war. One came with the arrival on Iwo of a troupe of performers from a big musical production in New York, sponsored by the USO, "Winged Victory." The cast from the original show was broken down into smaller groups of players called "Winged Pigeons," and they went around the world entertaining servicemen.

An accordionist, a singer, and a dancer spent a day entertaining us on Iwo. The accordionist was a lovely young woman. After the performance held on a makeshift stage on the runway, I talked to her. She was the first girl I had spoken to in a long time. We walked to a bombed-out Japanese bunker near the field and sat on top of it for an hour or more talking.

While we were together, I was completely detached from the war. We talked about her music. When she asked me if I had a girl friend, I told her about Doris. I remember asking her to call Doris for me when she returned to the States. I don't know if she did. I was impressed that women like her made trips into combat zones to entertain the troops. There were no accommodations for them on Iwo, so they flew back to Guam after several performances, including a few closer to the fighting than our airfield.

When it was time for her to leave, she signed my "short snorter" (a dollar bill signed by the first person who saluted us on the day of our commission). I still remember her name, Pat Meisenger, and the fact that she lived in Washington State.

As I sat in my living room remembering the war, I could see her and feel her presence, the khaki blouse and pants, the smell of her perfume, her soft voice.

Each of us had dug a foxhole when we landed on Iwo, but the ground officers had more time than the pilots to enhance their living quarters. Max Marshall, the Armament Officer, and Joe Delahunty, the Adjutant, shared a hole. They found a method of "extracting" wooden planks from the Navy and lined their foxhole with them. They even created shelves for their cans of rations.

One night, in the middle of a mortar attack, Max cried out "I'm hit! I'm hit!" Doc Lewis rushed over, then started laughing so hard he could hardly contain himself. A piece of shrapnel had hit a can of beans on the shelf, and the beans had leaked onto Max's shoulder. He had reached up, felt something sticky, thought it was blood, and started to shout. Max never lived it down. He was a good friend, an important member of the squadron because he was responsible for arming our fighters. What we thought of as an airplane, he thought of as a gun platform.

On a mission over Atsugi, I started down to strafe a hangar, fired my guns, then turned toward an airplane attempting to take off. As I came in range, I pulled the trigger, and not one gun fired. There I was in a position to kill an enemy, but I didn't have any guns that fired. My anger cooled on the long flight home. Max and I had a serious discussion about what happened. A few days later he informed me that he had loaded a new batch of ammunition into my plane without first testing it, and it was all defective.

One morning in early April, Doc Lipshitz, our group dentist, came up to me and said, "grab your helmet and get in my Jeep."

"Where are we going?" I asked over the roar of the motor, as we headed for the foothills of Mount Suribachi.

"To a Seder," he shouted back.

I thought he was joking. It was Passover season, but the idea of a Seder seemed too incongruous there on this war-torn island in the Pacific.

It turned out to be true. The Marines had arranged for a shipment of matzos to be brought ashore and an altar to be set up, under heavy guard. A Marine Chaplain conducted a short ceremony in Hebrew, while all the Jewish soldiers who had gathered listened from their foxholes. The rhythm of his chanting rose and fell, sometimes clear, sometimes inaudible below the sounds of the machine gun fire and the boom of the big guns shelling the shore from the sea.

A Seder is generally quite long and accompanied

by specific foods, such as matzos, a flat, unleavened bread, symbolic of the hasty flight from Egypt by the Hebrew slaves. Our ceremony was short, but, because of the setting, it was intense and moving. I hadn't observed my religion back home, before the war. But that Seder meant a lot to me and to all the men who attended it. I thought it spoke well for our military to arrange this ceremony in the middle of the fierce fighting.

After the ceremony most of the Marines returned to the front line units and more fighting, while Doc and I went back to our flight area. Later that afternoon I flew a patrol mission.

War was a twenty-four hour, seven-day-a-week occupation. The only rituals or observances were Sunday prayers for Christians at the portable altar and Friday night services for the Jews in a foxhole. We held memorial services for the dead when we knew that someone was not coming back.

One day a P-47 that had been badly shot up over Japan needed to make an emergency landing. They didn't want the pilot to make a belly landing and tear up the asphalt runway on the second airfield; that runway was used for emergency landings for the heavy B-29 bombers. So they diverted him to make his crash landing on the dirt runway of the number one field.

When you landed a fighter, you routinely slid the canopy back, so that you could get out quickly in case of an emergency. This P-47 was so badly shot up that the pilot couldn't get his wheels down or his canopy open.

As he made a belly landing the airplane veered off to the left, hit an embankment, and caught on fire. We saw the pilot struggling to get out. Before the crash crew could get to him, the airplane went up in flames. We had to stand and watch him burn, struggling to get out of his plane. I walked away, thankful that it wasn't me and never gave it another thought. As I think about that now it sounds so heartless. But then, had we dwelt on all of the conditions that could happen to us, none of us would have ever flown again.

A weather condition on Iwo Jima called a temperature inversion caused a lot of problems, and one of the more miraculous events I saw during the war as well.

In April and May, the temperature of the ocean and the temperature of the land was the same. This caused a thick ground fog, particularly in the mornings. Since the fog only reached up ten to fifteen feet off the ground, it didn't prevent us from taking off, because in a few seconds, we were above it. But we couldn't land in it. It was so thick that, from above, we couldn't see the ground to find the runway. We couldn't take a chance flying into it, because we never knew how deep the fog was, where it would end, or when we would suddenly hit the ground.

On our missions to the Japanese mainland, we would take off in the early morning ground fog and be gone for seven or eight hours. Usually the sun would have burned off the fog by the time we got back. But on one mission, the fog didn't burn off by the afternoon. As the planes began their return, visibility was clear until they neared Iwo. Below them the island was covered by a solid blanket of impenetrable fog.

A decision was made that every pilot on the mission would bail out as he reached the island, and those of us on the ground would be posted along the shore at fifty foot intervals, to act as spotters. We would try to see parachutes coming down, or splashes as men hit the water, so that we could direct the rescue efforts. All the planes would be lost, but the pilots would be saved.

Just a few minutes before the planes reached Iwo Jima the fog suddenly lifted. Half an hour after the planes landed, the fog was back. It happened just like that.

By mid-July, Japanese fighter opposition had virtually disappeared. Our intelligence forces told us that the enemy were saving precious fuel and planes to repel the invasion they knew was imminent. We spent our time over Japan searching for targets to rocket and strafe. On several of these missions, I shot up the shipyards at Numazu and strafed Atsugi. On one mission, I started down to strafe a train. As I began my run, the smoke from the trains engine belched out faster and faster as the engineer poured on more power. Before I fired one round at the speeding train, it came to a curve and couldn't make the turn. It kept going straight, right off the tracks.

Our preferred tactic against the more maneuverable Japanese airplanes was to make a high speed pass and break down and away to the right. That way we could escape, climb at high speeds, and attack again. The Zero, with its large, radial engine, could not turn to the right at speeds above 300 mph. Below that speed, it could turn inside of the P-51.

One afternoon, I hit a Zero pretty badly. As I closed in, I saw that the plane was falling apart. The pilot bailed out and came within a few feet, literally, of hitting my airplane. I could see the startled expression on the pilot's face, the disbelief that this was happening to him. For a split second he floated by me, hanging in the air, his plane in flames and shattering in the background. I didn't see his chute open, I was going too fast and really wasn't concerned. His plane was on fire and that is what mattered.

We knew the invasion of Japan would happen soon, and that casualties would be high. Our intelligence people were estimating that more than one million Americans would be killed or wounded. Our motto became "Back Alive in '45." But many of my friends would not be able to live up to the motto.

CHAPTER
ELEVEN

Losing Friends

WHEN WE JOINED the 7th Air Force, we had passport-size identification photos taken. I collected these small pictures from most of my squadron mates, and kept them with me throughout the war. When I came home, I put pictures of the friends who didn't make it on one page in my album.

Now, as I sat looking at their pictures, I saw them all as young men and cried for them as I had never done before. I sat there and sobbed.

I wondered what power or fate allowed me the gift of life and decreed for them a youthful ending, a cancellation of their futures? Not one knew marriage, family or grandchildren. All were under twenty-three years old.

Even though forty-five years had passed, I could recall all the pilots of the 78th who were killed, and the circumstances of their deaths. Some were classmates I had known from the time I became a cadet in 1942. Some were newcomers, gone before I had a chance to get to know them.

Major Bill Southerland was the first, followed by Howard Edmonson, Bob Ferris, John Lindner,

Bargaehr, Mathis, Wayland, Wightman, Carr, Sherren, Westlund, Williams, Schroeppel, White, and finally Phil Schlamberg. All in their early years, all for the love of their country, all in a war with an enemy who is now our "ally" and "friend."

John Lindner, Ed Green, and Bob Ferris were killed in training accidents. Lindner killed himself trying to find out how fast he could go in a Mustang. Ed Green died when his P-47 went into a flat spin. And then there was Bob Ferris.

On a bright, cloudless day in November 1944, I was watching a flight of P-51s doing string aerobatics over Bellows Field on Oahu, when a young sailor came up to me.

"Do you know Bob Ferris?" he asked.

"I do, but I'm sorry, you can't talk to him right now," I said, and pointed to the last plane doing loops overhead. "He's right there." Just then, Bob began a dive to gain enough speed to do a loop. He was the last man in the sixteen-ship formation and needed considerable speed to get over the top and maintain his position.

The Mustang was a sensitive airplane at high speeds. It required a delicate touch on the controls and complete co-ordination at all times to prevent buckling the skin or pulling off a wing. As we watched, Ferris's P-51 exploded into tiny pieces of glistening metal. Chunks of aluminum the size of plates came down from the sky, sparkling in the sun. Nothing was ever found of Bob's body. All that could be reclaimed was his helmet. The sailor standing next to me was

Bob Ferris's brother, in from a combat tour on a cruiser.

A day or two later, four planes crashed into Rabbit Island, off Oahu, one after another. Four pilots lost. We were becoming hardened to the realities of war. People died, even in training. The pilots were expendable, the machines difficult to replace. That was the message that came down to us from headquarters.

Of all my squadron mates who were killed, I knew Al Sherren the best. By today's standards, Al was a small fellow, no more than five foot six. He came from Waterloo, Iowa, and with his blue eyes and straight, light brown hair, he looked as if he had just walked out of a field of tall midwestern corn. Al was a year or two older than I. He had a keen sense of humor and often spoke of his home and family. We were all smokers at the time. I smoked Chesterfields, Al smoked Luckies. Whenever he asked me for a cigarette he would look at it and throw it to the ground. "As bad as I want a smoke I won't smoke these," he would say. In time I switched to his brand. I remembered how he would turn his cap around and pretend he was a German submarine officer at a periscope. Whenever we were down, Al would find a way to make us laugh.

Al had gone to high school with the five Sullivan brothers. In one of the great tragedies of the war, all five were killed when their Navy ship was sunk by the Japanese. The military had regulations forbidding members of a family to be on one ship together, but the Sullivan boys had requested special permission to serve together, and had received it. All the boys in the family were gone in one stroke.

Before the War, while he was still in school, Al had worked for the National Cash Register Company. Al and I often talked about what we would do after the war, when the fighting would be over, and we went back home. I didn't have much of a clue then, but Al did: he was going to finish school and become an engineer; they were holding a job for him at NCR.

Al and I met in Phoenix in 1942 when we were cadets at Luke Field receiving our Advanced training. We went through flying school together and joined the 78th Fighter Squadron at the same time. Al's hatred for our enemy was as great as mine. We had been friends for nearly three years when he was killed over Tokyo, on July 8, 1945.

He and Bob Carr were both killed on that day. We heard Al call, "Mayday, Mayday, I'm hit. I can't see." Then silence. Not one of us heard a distress call from Carr. No one saw their planes go down. They just disappeared.

When I came back from the mission, the personal grief of war struck me. My friends, Sherren and Carr were gone. It was an emotional, difficult time for all of us. We had to pack up their clothes, put them in their footlockers, and ship them back to the States.

Before the war, I had never seen dead bodies. I had never even been to a funeral. Nobody in my family had yet died, and I didn't know what death meant. But now, I knew that if I thought about my good friends and felt too sad for any length of time, I could never get up in the morning and fly. I just did not think too much or let myself feel much about them. So the deep feelings were buried and did not surface until much, much later in life.

We fliers shared months, sometimes years together, but we always knew it was nothing permanent. Death could take any of us at any time. All through the war that was our experience: to be close to people, to share combat with them, to know every day that you could get killed, or they could get killed. There was little opportunity to mourn the death of a fellow pilot, or to heal your heart from the loss of a friend; there just wasn't time.

Danny Mathis and I were friends. He was a gentle, soft-spoken man from South Carolina. We became close friends in Hawaii when I was the squadron Athletic Officer. He played shortstop and I played second base on our squadron softball team. Danny was a terrific ballplayer. Short, fast, with good hands and a fine bat. He was a tough competitor. Our team won a lot of games.

We made a good double-play combination. At times, it seemed we could read each other's minds. Later, when he flew on my wing, he seemed to anticipate my moves before I made them.

Danny flew on my wing a number of times, both in training and later, on Iwo, in combat. He was an able, competent pilot. On May 29, 1945, we combined to shoot down a Japanese Zeke fighter over Tokyo. The next day Doc Lipshitz, the group dentist, pulled all four of my wisdom teeth, and I was grounded. Danny was assigned my place, in my plane, the Dorrie R.

One hundred seventy Mustangs from three fighter groups left Iwo Jima on an escort mission on the morning of June 1. They were to join four hundred fifty B-29s on a massive raid against the industrial city of Osaka. As usual, a B-29 was assigned to escort the fighters and serve as navigation/weather airplane. Several hundred miles from Iwo, a huge weather front loomed ahead of the fighters. The lead B-29, unaware of the capabilities or limitations of the P-51s began a climb to get over the front. The Mustangs, unable to keep up with their escort, closed formation and entered the turbulent weather.

Visibility was so limited that it was difficult for wingmen to see their leader only five feet away. One of the squadrons followed their leader down to 5000 feet where they broke out of the storm. Another tried to climb over the top and met with moderate success. A few of his planes spun out of control, taking others with them. The 78th, led by Jim Tapp, flew through ice and snow, finally emerging at 22,000. Not one of the squadron leaders heard the call to abort the mission. Those that penetrated the front and reached Japan, were forced to fly through it again on the return to Iwo Jima. In all, twenty-seven P-51s went down. Only three pilots were recovered—one of them after four days in a life raft.

At the debriefing, all of the pilots reported similar experiences inside the front. Turbulence knocked out their gyro instruments, forcing them to fly, some for two hours, on the basic needle, ball, and airspeed. All reported vertigo, their mind and body reporting a different flight attitude than the instruments. It took

great faith and consummate skill to maintain straight
and level flight. One pilot, breaking into a clear area
between clouds, saw a P-51 flying directly at him but
upside down. He didn't know who was right side up
until he reached for his shoulder straps to see if they
had any slack. Danny was one of the two pilots from
the 78th who was lost. Jack Nelson was the other. An
investigation revealed that several B-29s assigned to
escort duty aborted, and a green, untried crew was left
in charge. From that day forward, an experienced
Mustang pilot was assigned to the lead escort plane
and was designated acting-command pilot. I flew in
that capacity on one of the first missions.

The terrible nature of war is that losing Danny
was hard, but losing my plane was shattering. I had
picked her up new at Hickam Field, just before we left
for combat. I had babied the engine during the break-
ing-in period. Joe Guldan, my crew chief, had taken
the engine apart and put it back together on more
than one occasion. We were a team: the crew, the
pilot, and the plane.

When I strapped myself into the "Dorrie R" I
knew she would take me to the target and bring me
back alive. I had Doris's picture taped to the instrument panel; my helmet was tucked away near the
throttle. Everything about the plane was familiar to
me: the throttle settings, the way she handled in a
dive. She was a tried and trusted friend. And now she
was gone.

It was a sobering thought that I was more affected by the loss of my weapon than by the loss of a
friend. What is it about war that makes a piece of

equipment more important than human life? I was so preoccupied with the loss of my plane, it was as if Danny never existed, yet, I wanted, needed, to have a plane to fly and fight my enemy.

Two of my wing men, Dick Schroeppel and Philip Schlamberg, were killed on separate missions. Because the flight leader and his wing man have a direct responsibility to protect and look out for each other in a flight, I've carried a feeling of guilt about their deaths for all these years, although I know there was nothing more I could have done to save them.

Dick Schroeppel also came from New Jersey, and we became quite close because of that geographical bond. Most of our fellow pilots chided us, quite regularly, as "Joiseyites." Dick was a quiet fellow, sort of a loner. Like most of the fighter pilots, he seemed confident and sure of himself.

He was following me down on a strafing run at Chichi Jima on July 3 when his plane was hit. He bailed out at a low altitude as soon as he was hit, and we watched him drop onto the rocky coast alongside the runway. A total effort to save him was immediately set in motion. We saw him get out of his chute and, using the rocks for cover, make his way to the rocky beach. Dick began swimming to the open sea as soon as he reached the water. The spray of machine gun bullets and mortar fire was all around him. Our P-51s strafed the gun emplacements along the edge of the field, and a B-17 arrived and dropped a large life boat in the open sea. Dick was seen to pull himself into it.

A full squadron of aircraft, on their way to Tokyo, was diverted to provide cover for a Navy PBY

"Dumbo" flying boat to attempt a rescue. We continued our strafing to give the pilot of the flying boat a chance to land and pick up Dick. But after getting down and taxiing up to the raft, the navy surgeon on board saw that it was too late.

Then, with Dick's body still in it, we were called upon to sink the raft so that the "Japs" couldn't get it. Dick was twenty-one. The Navy flying boat pilot was later awarded the Navy Cross, the nation's second highest medal, for landing in the harbor amidst all the shelling.

That experience made me proud of the people and the values for which I was fighting. Because our culture believes that each individual life is precious, a large number of men, and a whole squadron of aircraft on its way to a bombing mission, became involved in a dangerous air-and-sea struggle to save one man. Every one of us gave all we had, willingly risking our own lives to try to save Dick. And things like this happened all the time. Everything stopped when somebody was in trouble. I think of this often now as I grow older and wonder why that feeling prevails only in war and not in peace.

Phil Schlamberg and I were not far apart in age, but he was a 2nd lieutenant, a new pilot, and I was a captain, a senior pilot with a lot of missions under my belt. What brought us together was that he was also Jewish, and I had a kind of big-brotherly impulse to look after him. Until Phil joined the 78th, I was the only Jewish pilot in the squadron. I felt the responsibility for his death even more because of our shared heritage.

Phil was almost too tall to be a fighter pilot. The maximum height was six foot one or two; if you were taller than that, you wouldn't fit into the cockpit of the airplane. Phil was the maximum height, skinny with a gangly walk. He was very bright and alert and spoke with a heavy Brooklyn accent.

When I met him he was really just becoming a combat pilot. The training command in the States taught men to fly but never trained them as combat pilots. In Hawaii, and even on Iwo Jima, we would get pilots who had never flown upside down in their training, and the ability to fly upside down was a crucial part of combat.

You didn't become a combat pilot until you went through thirty or forty hours of "hand-to-hand" individual air-combat practice against more experienced pilots. We all honed our skills and learned the capacity of planes doing sixteen-ship formation acrobatics. You had to learn to depend on those sixteen men, to trust them, and move with them. If one man made even a small mistake, the whole flight could be in jeopardy. Until you mastered these things, you were just an individual who could fly an airplane, not an integrated member of a combat flight team.

Phil Schlamberg was just making the transition to combat flying; he had only flown two or three local missions, the fateful, aborted mission to Osaka and a few flights over Japan.

Phil had a premonition about his own death. He felt strongly that he should not fly on that last mission. When he told me how he felt, I spoke to our commanding officer and asked for a replacement. None was available. We were only allowed to fly a specific number of hours each month and most of the pilots had exceeded their quota. The only person who could get him off of the mission was Doc Lewis and then, only for medical reasons. Doc found nothing wrong with him, and the squadron leader did not have a replacement. So Phil flew.

At the briefing we were told that several B-17s would be airborne to act as radio stations. "We will broadcast the code word 'Utah' if the war ends before you hit the target. Abort the mission the minute you hear that signal," the intelligence officer told us.

Before take-off, I told Phil to stick close to my wing the entire mission. We flew to Japan, strafed our targets successfully, and started for the coast and our return flight to Iwo. Phil was on my wing the entire time. When we reached the ocean, I looked back and Phil was gone. No one saw him get hit or heard a distress call. When we returned to Iwo at the end of that mission, we learned that the war had ended while we were strafing Japan. None of us heard the signal that the war had ended.

Phil Schlamberg was nineteen years old when he was killed over Japan on the day the war ended. Quite possibly, he was the last American killed in World War II. Shortly after I returned to the United States in 1946, I called on his family.

I will never forget that day. The Schlamberg family lived in Brooklyn. Phil was the youngest, the only son, with seven older sisters. I had a hard time composing myself before I rang the doorbell. The family was gathered in the living room. His distraught mother was seated by the fireplace in a deep, high-back chair. She was sobbing, and when I approached her, she said, "It should have been you, it should have been you, not my Phillip." She was inconsolable the entire time I was in their home. One of the sisters apologized for her mother and asked about Phil, what kind of a pilot was he, how was he killed. I stayed for an hour. As I was leaving Mrs. Schlamberg told me, "You shouldn't sleep like I can't sleep."

I sat on the stoop a long time before I was able to get in my car and drive home.

As the war dragged on, the feeling of adventure and youthful exuberance faded into distant memory, replaced by our daily struggle to survive. One mission followed another, each one dangerous, each one possibly the last.

We were a tired bunch of fliers. Most of us had been on Iwo since early March. All of us had flown several missions over the Japanese mainland. We were living on Benzedrine and coffee and rumors about the end of the war, which were heard every day.

So far, I had been lucky. The casualty rates were high and getting higher, even among the more experienced pilots. We lost a large percentage of our squadron in those seven months of combat. But we didn't actually think of them as gone forever. I believe many of us thought of them as living somewhere else, and maybe we would see them again, after the war.

But at the end of the war we didn't see them again. As the years go by, I often think about these soldiers as young men. I remember what they looked like and their dreams for the future. In the pictures of them, the ones in my scrapbook and the others that I carry in my mind, they are vibrant, young, alive guys. They would have had families, they would have had all the things that I have, and I often wonder, why did they die, and not me? What did they do wrong, or what did I do right? Why did it happen that I lived and they didn't? I've had over forty-five years of life that they haven't had. They never got a chance.

For years I received invitations to our squadron reunion. I never went. I didn't want to be reminded of the war, to see the older faces of my friends. I wanted to keep their memories as young men fresh in my mind. I didn't want to talk about those who died. Whether it was guilt for my being alive when so many had died, I am not sure. I do know that I never expected to die in the war, and I suspect that those who did, felt the same way. Now, as I reflect, I think I was just lucky, never in the wrong place at the wrong time.

CHAPTER
TWELVE

———

Home from War

IN OCTOBER 1945 I received orders to fly to Guam, where I was processed to go home. The journey from Guam to Long Beach, California took twenty-eight days. Unlike my trip to Guam on a carrier, this passage was made on a large troop ship. Officers were assigned to rooms by rank, twenty or thirty to a room. We each had a bunk and a footlocker. I had taken my gun-camera film with me when I left Iwo and showed it one night as entertainment. The next day it was stolen from my footlocker.

On the ship I spent a lot of time with Colonel Mike Raymond, whom I had met on Guam. We played bridge every day and many nights. Both of us were bored and had a hard time sleeping. On one occasion we gave the cook fifty dollars to prepare some fried chicken for the two of us. The cook gave us a half-dozen cooked chickens. Mike and I felt like millionaires, taking a bite of a piece of chicken then throwing the rest of it over the rail.

When we got to Long Beach, a bus took us to March Field in Riverside. My only thoughts were of Doris and seeing her. As soon as we were processed, I changed my clothes and took off!

She was even more beautiful than before. When we first met, I must have seemed glamorous to Doris, because I was a pilot, or at least, an aviation cadet. But I had only been an eighteen-year-old boy who had just graduated from high school when I left, and now, two and a half years later, I was a combat veteran with a thousand hours in the air. My vision of war had come and gone, and I was faced with an uncertain future.

Doris was now a sophisticated young woman, in her last few months of college. She wanted to pursue a career as an actress in New York. I was just glad to be home.

There wasn't much chemistry left between Doris and me, and there was absolutely no talk of marriage or any kind of future together. It had been a war-time romance, and now the war was over.

When I got back to March Field, I found a note on my bunk from Mike Raymond, along with his Colonel's leaves. "Your name was called to get on a plane to go home," the note said. "Rather than cause problems, I went home as Jerry Yellin. Here's my leaf. You go home as Colonel Raymond." And that's what I did.

It had taken three and a half years for me to go from civilian, to cadet, to pilot, to combat pilot...but it took just three minutes to go back to civilian status. I was discharged a Captain on December 10, 1945.

When I arrived home my mother and father acted as though I had been away at college or on vacation. I had to wear my uniform so my father could show off the medals, the wings, the stripes that I had received for overseas duty, my Captain's bars. They never asked me, "What did you do over there?" "How was it?" "How do you feel?" Nobody asked me about the war.

My father wanted to show me off in my uniform, and I wanted to forget. I went to New York with him on occasion, in full dress uniform. Once, in line at Lindy's, a famous restaurant on Times Square, the maitre d' spotted me at the end of a long line and waved me to the front of the line. My father was so proud, and I was slightly embarrassed. The other patrons applauded as we were seated. The next day I gave my flight jacket, helmet, goggles, and uniforms to some youngsters in the neighborhood.

The first year after the war, I wandered. I went to California twice. The first time I went to see Doris, in the hope that maybe, after all, there could be something between us. When I realized that there was nothing there, I returned to New Jersey. Then a cousin called and offered me a job in construction in California, so back I went. On that trip, I met a girl and stayed for a few months, but it didn't work out: not because of the job or the girl, but because I couldn't settle down.

My mother tried in her own way to help me find my place, a vocation, something I might enjoy doing. She sent me to a number of universities for psychological testing or career counseling, to see what I should be and what I should do. "Why aren't you this?" she would ask of me. "Why aren't you that?" I always thought there was something wrong with me. She took me to a vocational counselor in Jersey City, who gave me some tests and recommended a profession and a college. Not once was the war mentioned, or my experiences. I began to feel that I wasn't normal.

As time passed, I began to feel that I would never be satisfied unless I had a cause. The war had given me a tremendous sense of purpose, of doing something important, for my country and the world, something that transcended my own little life and gave it meaning.

For years I was restless. I tried different businesses, different careers, different places to live. I never felt that I belonged, anywhere, no matter where. Soon after I arrived home, I took a job selling advertising. One day I met a general from the 7th Air Force on a bus in New York. I recognized him from a briefing I had attended on Iwo. When I introduced myself, he asked me to come with him. "I'm meeting a man who wants to start an airline," he told me. A few hours later I was hired as a pilot for Trans Caribbean Airlines. For the next year I flew DC 3s to Miami and Puerto Rico. It was terribly boring after flying fighters.

In 1948 I thought about flying fighter planes for Israel in their fight for Independence. My mother talked me out of it. Then in 1965 I went to Israel to play golf in the Maccabiah games—a competition much like the Olympics, held every four years for Jewish athletes. I thought I had found a place to live that would give my life more meaning. I took my family to Israel to live in 1966, still searching for that purpose, that cause. But it wasn't in Israel as I had expected.

In the ensuing years I worked for a building company and eventually had a career in land development as a builder/developer of summer homes in New Jersey. In 1967 we moved to Florida, and I spent seven years working for developers before I started my own company. In time I became an advisor to banks and somewhat of an expert in problem loans. It was that knowledge that led me to Japan in 1982. We were asked to present real estate opportunities in the United States to the Mitsui Bank in Tokyo. In 1985 I became interested in computers and finished my business career marketing computer software across the country.

The only satisfaction I got out of my life for many years was playing golf. I could be alone with myself, and it was something I did well.

Saturday was my favorite day of the week, the only day that had any meaning. It was mine to do as I chose. This feeling lasted for many years, almost my entire life. Of course, my family, my wife, and children were always important to me. But outside of them, I couldn't seem to connect with anything meaningful. Just working to make a living, to make money, was a duty, not something I was ever excited about.

The feeling of purposelessness has left me now, quite late in life. The change began shortly after I saw *Platoon* and cried about the war for the first time. The feeling of purpose has grown tremendously as our children have become parents. In fact, I now feel that there was purpose to my life all along, that I just did not recognize what it was.

I have often wondered how any government can ask its citizens to fight in combat and then expect them to lead a natural life afterwards. People who do unnatural things are affected for life. They can't go back to being what they were.

For many years, I wouldn't allow myself to feel the pain of the war. I couldn't face it. I didn't even know I had it. If I had felt the pain, if I had taken care of it when I was younger, perhaps I would have had a different kind of life.

I married, had children, did the best I could to enjoy the pleasures of life and take care of my family. But the war never left me. I didn't think about it or talk about it, but it was there inside me all along, living its own hidden life.

Alone, late one night, looking at the pictures in the scrapbook, I cried again. For Danny, and Al, and Phil, and Dick, and the rest. And for myself. I had returned from the war scarred beyond imagination, and never knew it. The restlessness I felt was the pain of my memories, deeply embedded in my soul. Memories that only now were surfacing. For the first time, I realized that the horrors of war had shaped my entire life. I wondered how many others had lived their lives as I had, under such a cloud of darkness.

Now the memories were no longer hidden; the buried feelings, all the pain and sorrow and mourning had risen to the surface. At last, after forty years, I felt a glimmer of peace within me. I finally let myself mourn for all of my friends who died for their country.

I slept soundly that night. In the morning I took my scrapbook to the Aerospace Museum in San Diego and gave it to the curator along with my medals and wings. I wanted nothing in my home that reminded me of my war with Japan.

Yas Takesue called from Los Angeles in July, 1987. "I am coming to San Diego on Thursday for a business meeting. Could we spend some time together?"

"Of course, Yas. Can you stay for the weekend?"

"That would be wonderful," he replied.

We arranged to pick him up at the station in Del Mar two days later. I was looking forward to reciprocating for his hospitality in Japan. Yas is a vibrant, personable, outgoing man who acts in America much like an American. He was dressed in sports clothes and carried a new golf driver that he had purchased in Los Angeles. I knew he would like to play Torrey Pines, so I had made a tee time for Saturday. When I told him, his eyes lit up, and he said, "I was wondering when I would get a chance to use my new driver."

Golf has been a craze in Japan, although a day of golf is expensive there compared to America. It costs a minimum of $100 depending on the location of the course. Some clubs near Tokyo cost $300,000 to $500,000 to join and have long waiting lists. As I traveled from Tokyo to Mishima on the train, I noticed golf driving ranges in every town we passed. The roofs of many office buildings had nets for catching golf balls.

When I visited a golf range near Robert's home, I was told that many golfers take out memberships in the range and have handicaps. Many Japanese "range" golfers have never been on a real course. Instead, they have tournaments at the range, hitting shots for accuracy and distance. One of Robert's elderly neighbors doesn't even belong to a driving range. Every Sunday morning he puts on his golf outfit, places a mat down in his driveway and spends an hour or two swinging his driver. On one occasion I gave him some tips on his stance and tempo, which he told me helped him a lot.

After our game of golf on Saturday, Yas and I returned to home for dinner. Helene had cooked pasta and mussels, a meal that Yas enjoys because it is not available in Japan. It was a lovely San Diego evening, cool and breezy on our porch overlooking the ocean. As we were admiring the sunset, Helene brought up the subject of marriage in Japan.

"We heard that most Japanese marriages are arranged. Isn't that so?"

"Not so much anymore," he replied. "In our culture, marriage is the joining together of families. In the past, all marriages were arranged by a go-between at the request of the head of the household. When it was time for a young man to get married, typically at the age of twenty-seven or twenty-eight, a go-between would be asked to find a young woman from a similar economic, social, and educational background. If the prospective groom was the oldest son, he would inherit the property and the business when his father passed on. His wife would be expected to take charge of the household and care for her husband's parents as they got older.

"In homes that had only daughters, the go-between would search for a man from a family of similar social and economic background. When a man was selected, and the ceremony performed, the bridegroom would then take the name of the bride's family as his own. This would ensure that the bride's 'house' would continue in perpetuity. In Japanese culture the family tree is called *ie*, which translates in rough terms to what you would call a family lineage. It is important to keep the family name alive because to lose it would be a discredit to all of the preceding ancestors.

"I think," Yas continued "that the strength of the Japanese people and nation stems from the continuity of behavior and customs that we learn as children within our homes. As young children we are taught the two sides of our world as we live it daily. One side is the *uchi*, or inside, and the other is the *soto*, or outside. These words translate to mean, 'inside and clean' and 'outside and dirty.' " He smiled.

"One of my first memories is of my grandmother scolding me for not taking off my shoes when I walked into her house. 'Shoes,' she said, 'are dirty; you must never bring them into your home.' In some houses clothes are also changed upon entering, and in others, hands are washed and mouths rinsed, so as not to bring germs into the living quarters.

"Within the home, the toilet room is separated from other parts of the house and is considered *soto*. When a person goes into the toilet, he or she must put on special slippers for use in that room only, and must remove them before entering the *uchi* area."

As he spoke, I smiled as I remembered an incident in Kyoto while staying at the beautiful Old Miyako Hotel on our first visit to Japan. We had decided to spend as much time as possible living Japanese style and had taken a room in the Japanese section. We were escorted into the room by a Kimono-clad woman and, as she pointed out the features of the room, Helene went into the toilet. When she came out she was wearing the bathroom slippers, not knowing she was supposed to take them off before walking on the *tatami* mat. The woman became hysterical, shouting in Japanese and wildly waving her arms. We were stunned for a moment until she pointed at the slipper-clad feet. Embarrassed, Helene sheepishly took them off and returned them to the toilet room.

I related this experience to Yas, much to Helene's embarrassment, and he laughed with us over it.

"Going back to the family closeness," said Helene, perhaps trying to change the subject, "your parents live near you, don't they, Yas?"

"Indeed they do," he said. "They are elderly and live in my neighborhood. I expect that they do not have a great deal of time left on earth. I have built a room in my new house for whomever survives, and I fully expect to have one of my parents move in when the time comes."

Mrs. Takesue's mother has been living with them for many years. When Yas built a new home, he built a small suite of rooms for her. She has her own kitchen

and makes most meals for herself, enjoying the priva-
cy elderly people want and need, plus the comfort of
companionship when she wants it. Yas told us that the
neighborhood has a community building that is fre-
quented daily by the elderly for all sorts of activities.
It is supported and kept up by the residents of their
neighborhood.

"We are taught," Yas continued, "that we must
never do anything to bring discredit to our 'house'.
Every action we take reflects directly upon our entire
lineage; backwards to our ancestors, here in the present, as well as into the future. We learn two types of
behavior as well. *Honne* means how we behave in our
uchi environment, and *tatemae* means how we are
expected to behave in a *soto* environment. This behavior is carried over into every aspect of our lives as we
progress in age. When we enter school our school
becomes an inside world and our classmates become
like family. We all dress alike and learn to take responsibility for our individual actions as well as our actions
as a group.

"We may seem, to the outsider, to be people who
are incapable of acting as individuals," said Yas. "That,
of course, is not so. In reality we are as individualistic
as any other nation of people. We just place much
more emphasis on living harmoniously. Our entire
existence is based on living in harmony with people
and our natural surroundings. It is the only way we
can survive in such a small land."

Yas's words triggered my memory. I thought back
to my first day in the army in 1942. With my GI (government issue) haircut and GI clothing, I looked like

everyone else. Quickly each of us lost all sense of individuality and started to become a unit. We learned to march in unison in small units, then larger units until we could join an entire brigade in dress parade. Our sergeants lectured us about military dress code, especially in wartime. Being out of uniform, having a part of your uniform askew, or not wearing your hat, might subject you to a court martial. The purpose of all of this military training is to turn men into machines.

After the war we took off our uniforms and went back to private life. The Japanese never take off their uniform. Their uniform is being Japanese and they wear if proudly at all times. They "march" in unison all of the time. To me that is the main difference between the United States and Japan; they are a nation of 125 million people who can "march" in tune with each other. Perhaps it is one of their great strengths but it is also one of their weaknesses. It gives them the same sort of identity that I had with all of my fellow servicemen, the sameness that built such great pride in "soldiering" for your country. We all knew what to expect from each other, how to behave in every circumstance, and how not to behave as well.

The Japanese wear their uniform well, both within their country and when they travel abroad. The structure of their country, of their industry, is built on that unique knowledge of expectation of their fellow men. They seem to know that they can count on promotions, pay raises, and prestigious assignments based on time served within the company; as long as the individual does not deviate too far from the approved track, just the way our civil service workers and military are promoted. It is that continuity of service that has created economic competition that is difficult for America to compete against. In Japan, competition is for market share which promotes quality in their product. In America, short term profit is the motivation for most businesses. It seems that Japan looks at long term profitability, and America looks at short term gains. The only negative to this is the lack of real, individual creativity within the system. The expression "the nail that sticks up must be hammered down" is the Japanese way of keeping harmony throughout their society, and it works well for them.

"I am telling you these things," Yas continued, "so that you can understand what is expected of Robert and why, in part, he has chosen to marry into a Japanese family. I have been his employer and friend for four years. He is one of hundreds of foreign students and teachers that I have had contact with in my business. When he first came as a visiting home-stay participant, he was older than any student we had ever accepted into the program. I was delighted when Robert subsequently wrote to me and asked me for a job teaching at Kiddy College. He has a depth of understanding, and a way about him that is almost Japanese. He is quiet and sincere. His students admire him as a teacher and as a person. Of course, he will always be regarded as a *gaijin*, a stranger, because of his appearance. Those of us who know him call him a *henna gaijin*—a stranger in looks but one who is knowledgeable in the ways of Japanese life. He has told me that he is more comfortable living in Japan than in America because of the orderliness he finds in his everyday life. He says that Japan is a country of few laws yet is a lawful society, while America is a country of many laws and is a lawless society."

"I know what you mean, Yas, I experienced the Japanese 'obedience to laws' myself recently. I had a reserved seat on the train to Mishima. It was quite late at night and the car was nearly empty, just a family of two adults and two small children sitting across the isle from me. They had turned the seats around and sat facing each other. A few minutes before the train left the station, a young man, perhaps twenty, came up to their seats and showed them his ticket. It was obvious that they were in his seat. Without hesitation they put the children on their laps and the young man sat down. They rode that way until we arrived in Mishima. I couldn't believe it, there were fifty empty seats in the car and neither party made a move to be by themselves. If I had been either party, I would have changed seats."

"That is not the Japanese way, Jerry. We are taught to obey all rules at all times. That boy's ticket was for a specific seat and the family was sitting in it, so they moved to their assigned seats. There can be no deviation from proper behavior in our view. What they did was quite appropriate in our society. This type of thing occurs often and is what has attracted Robert to the Japanese life style. It is not surprising to me that Robert and Takako are going to be married in a Shinto ceremony. Mr. Yamakawa is a religious man, and Robert has a feeling for what is proper. He expressed all of these things to me when he asked if I would be his go-between and speak to the Yamakawa family for him."

I reflected on the many times Robert and I had spoken about religion in our lives. I had moved away from traditional religious thinking and had adapted a much more universal approach to life. For eighteen years Helene and I have been meditating and studying the philosophy of life and death from an eastern perspective. Since he moved to Japan, Robert has learned about Zen Buddhism from a priest in a temple near his home.

I believe that mankind has to find a way of life that is meaningful and productive to the individual, without being harmful to our environment. I feel most at home living close to the land. When Robert told me that he was comfortable with his life in Japan, I thought I understood. But it wasn't until I spent time with him in Japan, saw how much at home he feels with the culture, spoke with some of his students and met some of his friends, that I knew why he feels the way he does. Some of his students invited us to their homes and gave parties in our honor. They asked us about Robert's life and adventures when he was young. It gives Helene and me great joy and pleasure when they tell us how much their *Sensei* (teacher) has meant to them. One woman, about fifty, told Helene that Robert opened her eyes to the world. "His teachings have exposed me to our culture and our environment in a manner that makes me want to know more about life in general and me in particular. I have begun to write because of Robert and become more active in my community. He is a good teacher, and we are friends."

Robert's best friend, Richard, is an Australian who also teaches English. He lives in a house adjoining a Buddhist temple on a hillside overlooking the rice fields of a small village. He acts as the caretaker for the temple in exchange for the use of the adjacent home. Richard spends two days a month in Zen meditation. He and Robert enjoy the hot spring baths at Shuzenji together and share a love for the spiritual aspect of life that permeates Japan. Helene and I enjoy Richard's company when we are in Japan and are comforted knowing that Robert has such a good English speaking friend.

One year we spent a New Year's holiday season with Robert and the Yamakawa family. It is the most important holiday of the year for the Japanese. They believe in beginning each year afresh, to pay off their debts, to thank their superiors for favors done and attention received, and to clean their homes. A few days before the holiday began, Robert and every other person in Japan began the ritual of "purifying" their homes. I hadn't seen anything like it since we were called for a "white glove" inspection in the military. Door tops were dusted, picture frames taken down and cleaned, ornaments and decorations removed and washed. Following this house cleaning, every car in Japan, at least every car that we saw in the neighborhood, was cleaned inside and out. Robert's neighbor actually removed the furniture from his home while they cleaned. Then they spent two days washing and polishing their two cars.

On New Years Eve we went to the local Buddhist temple at 11:15 P.M. to ring the temple bell at midnight. There were a hundred or so people of all ages in front of us. Unlike the west, Japan celebrates the New Year as a cleansing time of the soul, symbolized by the ringing of the temple bell 108 times—once for each sin of man, according to the Buddhists.

On or about the 15th of December, the New Year post cards are mailed. They are held by the post office and all delivered on the first day of the New Year. Robert received ninety-eight cards. He spent most of New Year's Day addressing cards to people that he had received from but not sent to. The post office in Mishima, a town of 100,000, handled three million cards. It is hard to imagine how many were mailed in the country as a whole.

While I was talking, Helene retired to the kitchen to make tea. When she returned Yas remarked, "I see you have some Bizen pottery, Helene, do you like it?"

"Very much, I enjoy the feel of the cups in my hand, and using my Bizen connects me to Robert. This tea pot and cups were a present from him on our anniversary last year."

"Some of Robert's friends are famous potters, many from Bizen," Yas injected. "In fact, Robert is becoming well known in Mishima for his pottery collection. A few months ago the local television station featured a tour of the *gaijin's* home, and we got to see how large that collection is."

Helene pressed Yas with more questions about Japanese weddings. "Can you tell us more about the actual wedding ceremony that Robert and Takako will be having?" Helene asked.

"Of course. Robert and Takako's wedding will take place inside a large temple building. The wedding ritual will consist of four elements: an offering, purification, prayer, and the drinking of *sake*. There is no wedding ritual similar to a western wedding just as there is no civil marriage in Japan. To get married in Japan, it is only necessary to register with the authorities.

"The ceremony within the shrine will include purification by a priest who will shake a decorated wooden staff over Robert's and Takako's heads. The marriage itself will be consummated when the two of them share a cup of *sake*. Afterward, you and the Yamakawas will drink together, and then the rest of the family in attendance. Through the ritual drinking of the *sake*, the two families will be united as one."

"But where does love fit in?" Helene wanted to know.

"Ah, so," Yas said. "A direct question from a western mother who does not yet understand our concept of marriage."

We all chuckled.

"We think that love and marriage in your culture is driven by sex. It is also our opinion that what drives western marriages also drives western divorce. You equate love as a sexual attraction; we equate sex as something that is a part of life. It is not really a reason to get married, but certainly a part of continuity of our 'house.' How is it possible," he asked, "to have love before marriage when you might meet your future wife only a short time before the ceremony? Even when men choose their own wife, the emphasis is on respect first. Respect for the continuity of lineage, respect for the woman's role in managing the home when he is at work, and respect for her as a manager of financial matters as well. Women in Japan are raised differently from women in America. And most men only tell their wives 'I love you' once, when they first get married." We had heard that before from Sen Matsuda. I wondered what women thought about that.

"Wait a minute," I said. I looked across the table at Helene. "I want to ask you a question. Why did you marry me?"

Helene looked puzzled for a moment and then replied. "I had just turned nineteen and wasn't very worldly. You were older than the boys I was dating. You were sophisticated, I liked the way you looked, and I recognized 'something' within you that I found appealing and attractive. You asked me and I guess I was ready."

"Interesting," I said. "You didn't say anything about love. You know, while Yas was talking, I couldn't help thinking about us. We have been married almost forty years and, if you don't mind, I'd like to tell Yas our story." Helene nodded her approval.

"A family friend, Esther Heller, visited my mother when she was in the hospital in 1949. Esther and her husband, Marty, both dentists, had been friends with my parents when I was born. Marty was my baby-sitter when I was two or three. The Hellers also knew Helene's family. Helene's parents had met them on a cruise ship and had become friends, and also patients, for many years. While at the hospital, Esther asked my mother if I was dating anyone. When she said no, Esther said 'I have a girl for him! She is young and pretty and comes from a good family.' In a way Esther was acting as a broker and go-between. My mother took the telephone number and gave it to me. Helene and I had our first date, a blind date, on good Friday in early April 1949."

"What's a blind date?" Yas asked.

"It is going out with someone for the first time, without ever having seen him before, and the meeting is usually arranged by someone else," Helene answered.

"I was attracted to you right away," I continued. "You were quiet, naive, not as beautiful as you are now but pretty, and you were very intelligent. I knew after that date that we would be married and I told my mother so. You came from a similar background and I was ready. Esther knew us both well and thought it could work out. And it did. We both had respect for each other, and our families. We came from a similar heritage. But . . ." I paused a moment. "I wasn't madly in love at the time. I knew you would make a good wife and mother, and you have. We didn't sleep together until after the ceremony. We learned about each other, and grew together more and more with time. When we needed advice, we often sought out Marty Heller. When David was born, Marty became his godfather. So you see," I said, "our marriage was almost arranged—almost pre-ordained—and it has been just fine. We made a commitment to each other and, in times of personal struggle, stood by each other. We tried and succeeded in keeping our family intact through it all. I don't think our story is unique for our day, but it certainly is not the way it is done in America today. Our story seems to be more Japanese, don't you think, Yas?"

I could see that Yas had enjoyed our interruption. Yas then continued, "Today, Helene, Takako is a girl. When she is married she will become a woman with a definite role to play in Robert's life. She may continue to work for a while, perhaps a few months, and then she will become a homemaker. If Robert and Takako are a typical Japanese couple, they will begin a family shortly after the wedding. Once she has a child, she will be a full-time mother. That has been the strength of Japan, the continuity of family.

"Of course things are changing now, especially in the cities. Women seem to be working later in their lives and not spending as much time with their children. I don't envision that for Takako though. Her life will be devoted to her family because that is what she has seen in her own family. She, too, has an obligation not to bring dishonor on her family. And she will be the manager of the household. If they have a traditional Japanese arrangement, when he is paid, Robert will give her his earnings. She will put aside money for education, food, vacations, and household expenses. Men learn to love their wives for all that they accomplish in their role as a woman. Japanese wives understand a man's needs and have been taught how to take care of them.

"So, Helene, the most important ingredient of a Japanese marriage is respect for the institution of family, continuity of lineage or house, obligation to one's duty as a man and a woman, and from that comes love. Does that answer your question adequately?"

Helene smiled, nodded shyly, and said "that is much as it was when I got married but not how we approach things in America today. Women seem to want a career more than they want to take care of a home and family."

"What is your role as go-between, Yas?" I asked.

"My responsibility as the go-between will be a lifelong obligation. I not only establish credibility for your family, I can also assume the role of godfather to children when they come, counselor to the couple should any problems arise, and I may be asked to be the provider of financial credibility for the purchase of a house. In our culture the introduction of one person to another by a third party is a serious undertaking for all concerned. It becomes an obligation of the person who is introduced never to do anything that will bring discredit to his benefactor. When I accepted Robert's request to speak for him I was saying to the Yamakawa family, you can check me out for I am in business, a member of the community, a homeowner, a respectable Japanese man. Should you find me accept-able, you can be assured that Robert will make Takako a fine husband or I would not have represented him. In the days of the *Samurai*, should there have been a breach in this faith, a man was expected to commit *hari-kari*.

"The customs of the Japanese wedding are quite different from yours," Yas continued. "It is Robert's responsibility, as the groom, to give six months of his yearly earnings to Mr. Yamakawa to help defray the cost of furnishing a home. He will also find a suitable gift for each of the guests at the wedding. I happen to know that Robert had one of his potter friends make special bowls as his gift. The bride's family is obligated to furnish everything necessary for the couple to set up housekeeping. Futons, blankets, sheets, pillows, tea-sets, and the like. They also make the wedding arrangements, send out invitations, and tell the invited guests how much money to bring as a present for the bride and groom. Actually, the money that is brought to the wedding will be used to pay for the reception, the hall, and the food. Anything that is left over will be kept by the bride and groom. In that way, there is no real burden on any one family to pay for the party after the ceremony.

"My role, as go-between, will be extensive, both before and after the ceremony. I will be responsible for introducing the families to one another. Since today's ceremonies are patterned after ancient rites, it is assumed that the two families have not met in a formal manner and will not do so until the day of the wedding. I will introduce the two immediate families at a small ceremony before we go to the temple. After the wedding ceremony is completed, we will all return to the hotel for a reception, dinner, and speeches. Robert has many friends who will not be at the temple but will be at the reception. It will be my duty to tell them about the two families.

"Robert also has to choose a family that will be his 'Honored Family.' This is generally a family that has been important in the groom's life. In this wedding, Robert's Japanese family has been chosen. Mr.

Yamamoto will have the honor of making the first speech at the reception.

"There will also be a Master of Ceremonies, to keep the reception party moving. Mr. Osada, Robert's good friend, will do that honor. The Master of Ceremonies controls the entertainment and speeches. He will call upon friends or relatives to speak or sing or dance at the reception."

CHAPTER
THIRTEEN

Yas

MY MIND WANDERED from time to time while Yas was telling us about Japanese weddings. I couldn't help but think about the past, about what I had experienced in the war. This was my first formal explanation of Japanese behavior and customs. What I was hearing was so different from what I had known about Japan when I was younger. Without thinking of the consequences, I suddenly blurted out something that stopped the conversation cold.

"Yas, how is it possible that a nation with such concern for human dignity and harmonious relations, could perpetrate such atrocities during the war?"

There was a moment of complete silence. Helene rolled her eyes back and shook her head in disbelief. I sensed her discomfort but said nothing.

Yas was shocked, I could see. This was the first time I had ever approached the subject of war with him. But there was no going back. Finally he spoke.

"Jerry, my friend, we are talking about your son's wedding and you suddenly want to speak about war?"

"I can't help it," I replied. "I look at you, see a good friend, hear about your culture, but in my mind

I see the faces of my young pilot friends. I am overwhelmed by the thought of the terrible experiences of
our soldiers in the Philippines, the Bataan 'Death
March', Guadalcanal; and I cannot understand any of
it. I have been to Japan three times since the war. I
have fallen in love with the country. On my travels I
have had wonderful, warm, human experiences.

"Once on our way to Kyoto, Helene and I were
in the green car, first-class reserved seats. At the first
stop, an elderly, frail man, accompanied by a younger
man and a beautiful woman, boarded the train and
headed for our car. They looked for their reserved
seats, found them, and both of the men sat down. The
woman, without a reserved seat, stood, even though
there were a few empty, reserved seats in the car. I was
not comfortable with this situation so I stood up, ges-
turing with my hand for her to take my seat. 'No, no!'
She shook her head, so I sat down again and she stood
for the three-hour trip to Kyoto.

"A few days later, while we were having breakfast
in the Japanese section of the Miyako Hotel, the three
people from the train walked into the restaurant. The
elderly man spotted me across the room. He left the
other two and slowly walked to our table. As he
approached a broad grin spread across his face. He
extended his hand toward me and shook my hand
warmly, looking me straight in the eyes. I was taken
aback by this gesture. I knew that Japanese custom did
not include touching in public or handshaking in general. The only explanation I could think of for his
behavior was my action on the train a few days prior.
I was touched by his genuine sense of warmth.

"I have had similar encounters all over Japan. It is hard for me to equate the gentility I have experienced here with the war. Yet, when I am in Japan, I can't seem to forget what I saw as a young man.

"My experiences in Japan have been extraordinary. I have come to think of Japan, not as a country, a place to visit, my son's home, but as a neighborhood in the world that Helene and I live in. I have come to feel that the Japanese people I have gotten to know, are a part of my extended family. I believe that Robert's wedding is a wonderful thing for all of us, and yet, I have never had an explanation of how the things that I have seen could have been done by such a seemingly civilized nation."

It was several quiet, discomforting moments before Yas asked, "What is the Bataan Death March? I have never heard about that."

"Didn't you learn anything about the war in school, Yas?"

"Only what my government wanted me to know. It seems that a full history is only written and taught by the victorious, not the losers. Please tell me about Bataan."

I was an aviation cadet when stories of the Death March on Bataan Peninsula and the atrocities committed there, reached America. What I heard increased my anger toward Japan.

"In April of 1942 about 20,000 American servicemen—soldiers, sailors, airmen, and marines—were captured in Bataan by the Japanese at the surrender of the Philippines. It was the greatest defeat ever suffered by a U. S. military force, but the worst was yet to come.

"The Japanese had set up a prison camp about sixty-five miles from where the men were captured. Over the next few days, the servicemen and about 50,000 Filipino civilians were forced to march there.

"For months our forces had been living on half or even one-third rations, sharing their food with the Filipino people while trying to defend Bataan against Japanese attack. Many were wounded, or sick with dysentery, malaria, beriberi. Ravaged by disease, exhausted and half-starved, they were in no condition for a sixty-five mile forced march through the jungle with little or no food or water to sustain them.

"Over six hundred Americans and between seven thousand and ten thousand Filipinos died on that jungle trek. But it was how they died that enraged me. Months after the Death March, a few soldiers escaped and told what happened.

"There was almost no food. The Japanese had expected and prepared for 25,000 men, and there were nearly three times that number, already weak from lack of nourishment.

"Men were beaten and bayoneted. Many of those who were too weak to keep up, or who fell from exhaustion, were buried alive by their own comrades, held at gun point by the Japanese guards.

"They would halt the marching columns in front of artesian wells, let the soldiers see the fresh water, and then force them to continue without a drink. The prisoners were routinely looted by the Japanese soldiers who took toothbrushes, pens, soap. One officer refused to surrender his wedding ring and had his finger hacked off by a Japanese guard. At one point, for no apparent reason, about four hundred men were massacred, cut to pieces by swords.

"These stories seemed so horrible that they were nearly unbelievable. But then, on Iwo, what I saw verified those stories, and increased my hatred for the Japanese.

"I saw a nineteen-year-old Marine whose hair had turned white overnight from the horrors he had experienced. I saw dead Marines who had their fingernails pulled out, young Americans, my countrymen, with their faces bashed in so the Japanese could get the gold from their teeth. The Japanese to me were inhuman, absolutely inhuman."

There was another long pause before Yas spoke. I could feel Helene's eyes boring into me, but I had not been able to stop myself.

"Jerry," Yas finally replied in a gentle voice. "It may be just a condition of mankind that makes these things happen. I will try to answer your thoughts in the best manner that I can. I am totally unprepared for such a question—especially at this time—but I will do my best."

He sat for a moment, thinking. Then he continued.

"My father did not serve in the military," he said. "He was a railroad worker in Manchuria at the time of the war, and I was born there in 1945. We returned to Japan in 1946 where I did my schooling, graduating from high school in 1963, at the age of eighteen. I had no desire to continue my education in a formal way. I wanted to travel and see the world; the United States, in particular."

"What," I interjected, "has this to do with the question I asked?"

"I must answer your questions in my own way, Jerry. Please be patient, and I think you will have your answers. When I am finished, I am going to ask you a question that I have wanted answered for a long time.

"I arrived in America in the spring of 1964, with two of my friends. We were determined to walk across your country and learn as much about America and her people as we could. We began our eight-month trek in Los Angeles. In the course of our journey, we visited Indian reservations in Arizona and New Mexico. We were curious as to why people were made to live in such conditions. The answers we were given did not satisfy us. At the time I thought I must find out more about this. We wound up in the southern U.S., and again we were confronted by a curious situation. I had never seen black people before. They, too, were living in conditions that I did not see anywhere else in America. Again I could find no satisfaction in the answers I received.

"Perhaps, I thought, it is because my English is not perfect that I do not comprehend what I am told. I made up my mind, then and there, that I would learn to read and speak English fluently, and find some of the answers for myself. And I did. I read book after book about American history. I learned about your Pilgrims and their relations with the Indians of America. I read about the war you fought with Great

Britain, that established your independence. And I read about how you needed more territory and started your move westward to the Pacific Ocean.

"In my studies I read about your cruelty to the native people who lived on the land you wanted. I learned about how you killed the buffalo on the plains, so that the Indians would starve to death. And I read about the treaties you signed with the people you conquered, but did not honor. I read about your General Custer and the atrocities he committed in the name of 'civilization and progress.' Then I learned about a 'Death March' of Indians called 'the March of Tears.' Not much different from what you described happened in Bataan. I studied your Civil War, and how brothers learned to kill each other for the right to own slaves. In my travels in your South, Jerry, I found the southern people to be unlike others in your country. They seemed more gentle, living in a manner consistent with traditions long established. I know Japanese businessmen who have returned from working and living in the South. They tell me they are more comfortable there than anywhere else in the United States. The people have manners in the South, they say. How, then, is it possible that such gentle people could kill and enslave others?

"Two books that are popular in Japan are *Gone With the Wind* and *Roots*. From them I learned of the traditions of the blacks in their native lands. Did you know, Jerry, that of the millions of slaves who were shipped from Africa to the New World, more than six million died on the boats, in chains, before reaching shore. Only one million arrived in the United States."

"Yas," I said, impatiently. "Your learning about America from these books is almost the same as my learning about Japan from reading *Shogun*!"

"Perhaps," he said. "*Shogun* portrayed a Japan of ancient times, as do all of these books. But they were based on facts of the times, and we both got a flavor of what was happening from reading them. I learned that slaves that were sent to Brazil retained their customs and culture, while slaves that were sent to America lost theirs in a very short time. Most of what the slaves in America knew about their past was obliterated in a few decades to make them more docile. What is so distasteful to me, as a Japanese person, is the thought that one human being could own another human being. Animals can be owned, but not humans.

"What I read about of your history, how you treated the people you conquered, was not consistent with the stories my father and his generation told me about how you treated the Japanese people after you conquered our country. He told me about the kindness of your soldiers, the food you supplied a starving nation, and his gratitude to America. My dealings with the Americans on my trip were warm and friendly. Many times we were invited to stay the night with strangers. Everywhere we went, we were given food and presents. We experienced America much as you are experiencing Japan now.

"I tried very hard," Yas said, "to understand how a nation of people could enslave other people for their own gain."

"Wait a minute," I said. "While you occupied Korea, you sent thousands of Koreans to work in war industries in Japan. You also enlisted 100,000 Korean women as factory workers, and when they arrived in Japan, you shipped them to the front as sexual objects for your soldiers. Today, the descendants of those Korean people living in Japan, number 600,000. Most were born in Japan, speak only Japanese, and yet are not citizens of your country. Isn't that slavery too?"

Yas looked flustered. Unable to speak for a moment, looking me straight in the eye said, "Yes, all of that is true. I cannot speak about it with authority. As a matter of fact, most Japanese sweep it under the table as if it does not exist. This is a blemish on our society that must be cured if we are going to be leaders of the free world.

"That is another subject, Jerry, perhaps at another time we can discuss it. I really want to continue my thoughts.

"While I studied, I read books about what Japan did in countries we conquered in the war. Books that were not available in my country. Books that I sent for, from America and England. And I found out that people who fight, and conquer, behave in a manner in which they normally do not behave.

"What we first learn as young children in Japan sets the tone for our entire lives. Every Japanese person, in the North and in the South, learns exactly the same things in the same manner. We all become attached to, then proud of our school, then our company, our neighborhood, and of course, our country. Within the confines of any of these institutions, we behave in a manner consistent with everything we have ever learned. In our homes we are protected by our parents who, in turn, had been protected by their parents. In return for that protection, we become obligated to take care of our parents when we become parents and they become grandparents. This same condition applies in the company where we work. We give the company our services, and in turn they take care of our needs throughout our lives. Within the structure of the company, we give respect to our seniors and gain the respect of our juniors. We have built a society of people who have loyalty, discipline, and pride, knowing that we will not be let down by our co-workers, senior or junior, at any time. That is the group mentality that makes us so strong.

"In America, I have been told, should a senior employee or manager walk into the office of a junior employee and find that person sitting gazing out of the window, he will berate and embarrass him for not working. In Japan we act differently. In the same situation, the Japanese manager would turn around and tiptoe out of the office, knowing full well that the junior employee was working out a problem relative to their mutual business interest. He would only interrupt if that employee, whose office he had entered, was working, not thinking. So, Jerry, we have a code of behavior and ethics for almost every situation. We know how to behave and what is expected of us throughout our entire lives.

"Now, my studies have told me a little about why we went to war. The military were convinced that someday Japan would be at the mercy of 'the white world'. It was evident, they said, that Japan was surrounded by Asian nations and those nations were under the control of caucasian countries. Since we depended on our relationships with the west for our oil, it was evident that any breach in our relations would cut off our source of energy. You remember what it was like in the States in 1974 when your oil supply was cut down by OPEC. What would your country have done if your oil supply was entirely cut off? What action would America take if Kuwait or the Saudis decided not to sell oil to you or they were put in a position of not controlling their own destiny?

"Maps of the world from 1930 that we studied in school showed that our military leaders were partially correct—we were surrounded by 'white' colonies. So we started out to build an Asian Co-Prosperity sphere of influence in our region of the world. As we conquered those countries, we made the people work for our good. The mentality of our military leaders was such that they thought anyone who fought for their country must fight to the bitter end and die trying to win. They thought that was the way of all people, because that was the way they had been trained to think. People who had been conquered could be used any way the victors wanted, they thought. So it was in your own country in the early days, and so it was forty years ago when we had our early victories. Apparently, that is the way men have been behaving from the beginning of time. It is why you have the memories you have, Jerry, and it is why I thought so harshly of your country when I studied your history books.

"For the past twenty years I have traveled to America at least once a year. I am familiar with a great many people; have visited many places and feel much towards America and her people, as you and Helene feel towards me and my wife Junko, and to Japan. Those feelings have come about because we have come to know each other well. I cannot imagine that the American people of yesterday, or the Japanese people of today, would have done what they did had they taken the time to learn about each other.

"We have always feared the white world; you the yellow world. You have destroyed many races of people who had beliefs other than your own. Much of your belief has to do with religion. The religions of Christianity and Judaism are entirely foreign to us. 'How is it possible,' we ask, 'that so many people have been killed because of their interpretation of what the white people say is the word of god?' How is it possible to explain Jews kept in slavery in ancient times, pleading to the Egyptians 'Let my people go!', and yet today those same Jews have not allowed the Arabs in Israel to have their freedom? How can Catholics in Ireland kill Protestants, and Protestants kill Catholics, in the name of what they believe to be righteousness? How can a nation—America—which calls itself a democracy, have national holidays that exclude so many of its citizens? Christian holidays like Christmas and Easter leave out every other religious group. Your Thanksgiving, I am sure, is not looked upon with much favor by the American Indian."

I was astonished by his knowledge and the subtle process of his mind. "Yas," I said. "I have no answers for your questions, no argument for your logic, but I get the message."

"I have no message, Jerry," he said. "I only want

to say that we in Japan live by a code of behavior to our fellow human beings that is ingrained within our lives by tradition and culture. We do not need laws of behavior that, if broken, will bring punishment to us forever. We behave as we do because it is the only way that we can exist together in such a small country. I think most Japanese have overcome their fear of the white race because of the close association of these past forty-three years. Our future together depends upon a tremendous awareness of each other, or we can have no world. Today we in Japan are a peace loving people.

"I hope," he said, "that I have answered some of your questions about our actions in the war. We looked upon anyone other than a Japanese person as somewhat subhuman. You did too. That does not make it right, and it leads me to ask you a question that I have never had the courage to ask before."

I was unprepared for his remarks.

"We in Japan believe that America would not have used the atomic bomb on a 'white' country, Jerry. You are the first person other than a Japanese that I have said that to. We are friends, and I trust and respect you. Can you answer my question? Is America a racist nation and, why did America drop the atomic bomb when you knew the end of the war was so near?"

Helene and I were shocked by his question. She looked at me, wondering what I was going to say. I needed some time to think. It was late, we had been talking for several hours, so I asked, "Could we talk about this in the morning, Yas?"

"Of course," he replied.

CHAPTER
FOURTEEN

The Bomb

I SPENT A restless night thinking about Yas's question. How could I possibly answer my good friend from Japan without damaging our relationship? After all, I carried a hatred of his country in my heart much of my adult life. As a fighter pilot, flying combat missions, anything my country did to attain a total victory had my blessings.

I flew over Tokyo on August 6, 1945, the day the bomb was dropped on Hiroshima. When we returned from our mission that day, Phil Maher jumped on my wing before the prop stopped spinning.

"We dropped one bomb and wiped out an entire city," he shouted.

I remember looking at him as if he was crazy. I even think I told him "you're nuts."

"No, Jerry it's true. The war is as good as over."

"I hope it is, Phil," was all I could reply. We went into the debriefing hut and learned that an atomic bomb had been dropped on Hiroshima. None of us knew what an atomic bomb was or where Hiroshima was located. It didn't bother me then that 80,000 people were killed with one bomb. After all, I had seen

Tokyo on fire in the spring of 1945 when 200,000 people were killed.

On August 9 the second bomb was dropped on Nagasaki. In total, 176,000 people were killed by two atomic bombs, less than the number that were killed by the bombs dropped by the B-29s on Tokyo on May 24 and 25. I wondered what difference it made how you killed? Whether you use 1000 planes over Tokyo or one over Hiroshima. Or a bayonet, a rifle, a flamethrower, bomb, or atom bomb—the weapons of war are not the obscenity—war is the obscenity!

There is no doubt in my mind that my life was spared as a direct result of the atomic bomb, as well as the lives of all my friends in the 78th. To have a weapon that could kill as many of the enemy with one airplane as that of 1000 airplanes, and not use it, would have been unthinkable in time of war. I believe that the use of the atomic bombs saved millions of lives, both American and Japanese.

For years I defended the American use of the bomb to my friends as a weapon of war that had to be used, that saved lives, mine included. But it bothered me now that I had to explain my feelings, the temperament of my country at the time, to a Japanese businessman who was born in 1945. Revealing my feelings, answering his questions about racism and the bomb did not come easy. Nor could all of my answers come forth at one meeting. I could only answer some of his questions today in Del Mar. Some of his questions would have to wait to be answered in his home in Mishima.

Yas was a good friend and I had put him on a spot.

He handled it well, I thought, but now I had to satisfy this gentle friend from Japan. In truth, Yas's question had filled my own mind many times since the end of the war. I had read a great number of books that touched on the subjects we had been taking about. Books by both American and Japanese authors. A friend, Jack Lambert, had written and published two books about the Pacific War. It was he who sent me a copy of an article about the Japanese plans for repelling any invasion by America. Over the years, I reached my own conclusions, and now, I hesitated but I felt I had to share them with Yas. Before I went to breakfast, I gathered a number of books and articles that contained materials relative to what I was going to say to Yas. I wanted him to read for himself about the invasion plans of the Americans and the defensive plans of the Japanese. I wanted him to study what had helped me reach my conclusions about war.

After a late breakfast, Yas and I walked to the porch. I was silent, deep in thought, for several minutes before I began my response. It would have been too simple, yet insulting to my friend, if I said what I felt as a young man: "You started it—we finished it!" I had to do more, so I began: "Yas, I must answer your question twice. Once as a pilot about to embark on a mission that could have cost me my life, and once as a sixty-four-year-old man who has formed some conclusions about the war he fought.

"None of us who were flying combat missions from Iwo Jima ever anticipated that a dramatic event, the bomb, would end the war. We were being prepared for an invasion of your country that would begin in November.

"As early as July of 1945, we had little or no air opposition over mainland Japan. In fact, we flew over the country looking for targets of opportunity without fear of heavy flak or ground fire. On several missions I strafed airfields, shooting at parked planes that later proved to be wooden mock-ups of fighters and bombers.

"After a five-day leave in Hawaii, we heard rumors about our impending role in the invasion. My squadron, the 78th, along with two other squadrons of the 15th Fighter group, were to be used as cover for the invasion. These missions involved long, danger-ous, over-water flying and fighting by tired fighter pilots. Many of us knew that our time could be run-ning out. Looking at the numbers, I had strong feel-ings that I might not survive the war. The more you flew in combat, in fact the more you flew fighters, the greater your chances were of being killed. In the sum-mer of 1945, I was the eighth oldest pilot in the squadron, by rank and time. I was twenty-one, a cap-tain, a flight leader with nineteen combat missions and one Japanese plane to my credit.

"We learned from a briefing that phase one of the invasion of Japan, code-named 'Olympic', would begin at Kyushu."

"How many troops were involved in these opera-tions?" Yas asked.

"It was much larger than anything previously attempted, including the invasion of Europe. I don't remember all of the numbers, but there were over a half million Marine and Army assault troops on three thousand ships ready to make the invasion. In all, one and a half million American soldiers, sailors, airmen, and marines would be involved in the operation, backed by some three million more servicemen in reserve. Only Americans were scheduled to invade Japan, none of our allies would take part.

"Once Kyushu was in American hands, the invasion of Honshu would begin. The goal of these operations was the unconditional surrender and occupation of Japan. We expected casualties in the millions on both sides, at least one million Americans could be killed or wounded.

"On July 26, 1945, the United States government issued the draft of a document called 'The Potsdam Declaration,' calling on the Japanese government to proclaim an unconditional surrender. In the declaration, the Japanese military would be called upon to lay down their arms, return all conquered territories to their rightful owners, accept a military rule of their country for a specified time until a democracy could be established, and reduce the role of the Emperor to a figurehead."

Yas said, "Yes. I am familiar with its contents. This is one of the few subjects we learned in our schools."

"In the early days of 1942," I continued, "shortly after Japan attacked Pearl Harbor, the United States Department of State held talks regarding the disposition of Japanese territories after victory was achieved. These talks continued into the spring of 1943 when, with Japanese domination of the Pacific stopped, American forces began to recapture Japanese islands.

In May 1943, certain that America would be victorious, President Roosevelt formed the Kirk Committee to explore America's position in post-war Japan. Debate about Japan's future in the world scene resulted in a document not unlike the one issued in July 1945. At times the debate was furious and heated."

I reached for a book on the coffee table, opened it to a section and showed it to Yas. It was several pages of testimony to the Kirk Committee by a Captain Pence of the United States Navy who argued that Japan should be destroyed both as a nation and as a culture. Captain Pence's exact words were:

> The Japanese are international bandits and not safe on the face of the earth. The only way to ensure peace is to destroy them. Japan should be bombed so that there is little left of its civilization, and so that the country cannot begin to recuperate for fifty years.

I read the passage to Yas, paused for a few seconds then continued reading Pence's testimony.

> Such drastic measures were necessary because this was a question of which race was to survive. White civilization was at stake. We should kill them (the yellow race) before they kill us.

"You see Yas, Pence went so far as to call for the elimination of the Japanese as a race. He believed that there was little in Japanese culture that was worth saving or that could generate international peace and friendship. According to Pence, and I will read his exact words again:"

> The Japanese accepted western civilization only recently and should not be dealt with as civilized human beings. The only thing they will respect is force applied for a long period of time. Because Japanese domestic conditions had created the country's aggressive behavior overseas, the only way to eliminate the threat would be to destroy it entirely, or possibly turn it over to China. In either case, Japan as a culture and as a power should cease to exist.

Yas and I continued to look at the document on the table. I tried to soften the blow of Pence's words. "You know, Yas, change a few words here and there and Pence might have been Hitler talking about the Jews. There were some who agreed, but the majority did not.

"I would like to believe that America today, as a nation, is not racist. But that is not so. Suspicion and distrust of those who are not white or, I might add, Christian, has prevailed for centuries. The reaction to Pearl Harbor in my country was 'The Japanese are yellow-bellied cowards.' This feeling prevailed throughout the war. Much was done by our government, to provoke in our countrymen, opinions of the Japanese as back-stabbing, buck-teethed monsters. I believed what I was told about our enemy as I am sure the Japanese believed what they were told about Americans."

"Is that why you put American citizens of Japanese background into concentration camps while those of German or Italian ancestry retained their freedom?" Yas asked.

"Sometimes governments make monumental mistakes, Yas. Mine and yours. Looking back, that was one of them. Yours was Pearl Harbor. Sure, they were Americans citizens, but our senior officials knew nothing about the Japanese and thought they might be a threat. Unfortunately, many in our government today still do not understand the Japanese.

"It just proves what we were talking about. By the way, Yas, something similar happened to my friend's family, in Japan. James Kagawa, a golfing buddy, told me this not too long ago. His grandfather was a wealthy farmer from Fresno. In 1940 he sold his farms and went to visit his family in Japan. When the war started the Japanese government confiscated his money and would not allow him to leave the country. They thought he might reveal information about Japan to the Americans.

"There are many in this country today who still carry the feelings about Japan that they had in 1941. Even though Japan lost the war, they claim, they won the peace. The Japanese couldn't capture Hawaii during the war, so they bought it when the war ended. There are many in America who still feel anger and hatred toward the Japanese. Many veterans and their families have never forgotten their losses. And then there are those who feel that Japanese economic achievements have cost Americans their jobs and their security.

"But racism isn't confined to America, you know. You yourself, Yas, referred to the controlling nations in Asia of that time as 'white'."

Yas nodded his head in agreement and added, "In

Japan today we still have problems accepting certain Asian people as being equal to the Japanese."

"According to the history I have read," I said, "the Sino-Japanese War was seen, in part, as an inner war to cleanse the Japanese mind of western influences and thought, not just an action to bring the Chinese into the realm of pan-Asianism. It was thought by some to be a holy war against western influence and the domination of the Asian world by the white race."

"We were always told that we were better than others," Yas remarked, "but as I grow older, I find that we are all much the same."

"So true," I replied, then continued. "Three days after The Potsdam Declaration was issued, the Japanese government broadcast its rejection to the world. It was then that the decision to drop the atomic bombs on Japan was made. Had the invasion of Europe in June 1944 failed, and had the bomb been ready, I am certain that the atomic bomb would have been used on Germany. I am just as certain that the bomb was used on Japan as a military weapon against an enemy, not a race.

"Do you have any idea what was going on in Japan at the time the bombs were dropped, Yas?" I asked. "Did you know how many of your citizens were enlisted to fight to the death?"

"Yes, Jerry, I have read about our preparations for the defense of our country. My father told me that all schools were closed and the children conscripted. All males from the age of fifteen to sixty were made a part of the military. They were trained and armed for the defense of our country, many with just bamboo sticks.

"Females from the age of seventeen to forty-five were also armed and trained. Even small children were taught how to strap explosives to their bodies and throw themselves under tanks. Close to thirty-five million people were armed and ready to lay down their lives for the Emperor and the Country." Yas paused for a moment as we both thought of the consequences of an invasion.

"Yas, an American journalist wrote after the war that Japanese forces numbering 750,000 were waiting for the invasion to begin on Kyushu. He stated:

> In every invasion by American troops against Japanese held islands, the Americans outnumbered them by two, and sometimes three, to one. Now the odds would be different. According to Japanese war plans, on the night before the invasion began, two hundred planes would take off on suicide missions against the fleet. While American ships were approaching Japan, an initial force of two thousand Japanese planes were committed to controlling the sky over Kyushu. Eight hundred suicide planes were prepared to attack the troop-carrying transports and two thousand more, in waves of two hundred to three hundred an hour, would attack the troop and cargo vessels. In addition to the air attacks, Japan had assembled midget submarines, human torpedoes, and exploding motor boats to attack from the sea.

"The Japanese Air Force expected to stop the invasion with massive attacks, which they believed they could sustain for ten days. Their goal was to stop the invasion before the landing. Should that happen, they reasoned, they would be able to negotiate a less-than-unconditional surrender. If the Americans landed and made headway, the entire population of Japan was prepared to fight to the end to save the nation.

"We were fortunate to have had the knowledge and capacity to build the two bombs we used to end the war. But for a strange twist of fate, the bomb might have been built in Europe by our enemies."

Yas raised his eyebrows questioningly. "How could that be?" he asked.

"Enrico Fermi, the father of the nuclear age was born in Rome Italy, in 1901," I said. "In 1934, he conducted the experiments that led to the splitting of the atom, without realizing what he had done. For this experiment he was awarded the Nobel Prize in physics and was given permission to leave wartime Italy to accept the prize in Sweden.

"Although he was a Catholic, he was convinced that Italy's racial laws would affect his Jewish wife and two children if they returned to Italy. He accepted the Nobel Prize and then left Sweden for the United States where he worked on the chain reaction that made atomic bombs possible."

Yas looked directly at me and said, "I wonder what the world would have been like today if the bomb had not been invented."

"There is no doubt that the war would have continued much longer," I answered. "Japan might have been invaded by America in the South and Russia in the North, and the map of the world as we know it would have been altered. It is entirely possible that Japan could have been divided in two. We might have had to fight communism in North Japan much as we did in Korea and Vietnam. Who knows?

"I have always wondered whether scientists and inventors would have continued their projects had they known how they would be used. If the Wright brothers have known that an airplane would deliver a bomb as devastating as those dropped on Japan, or any bomb for that matter, would they have continued? And Fermi. . . was his vision of nuclear fission just the natural, progressive, development of science from his predecessors?

"For me," I said, "the answer to the question certainly brings to mind more questions than it does answers. For instance, would the bomb have been developed if Japan had not bombed Pearl Harbor? Even more, did the United States let Pearl Harbor happen, in order to have a reason to enter the war in Europe? Without the United States taking an active role in World War II, it is entirely possible that Germany could have prevailed. The temperament in our country at the time was one of 'America first; let's stay out of Europe'. Apparently President Roosevelt was a man of vision who knew we would have to become involved in the war. Had Germany won in Europe, and Japan been successful in Asia, America would have been the next target for invasion from the east and the west.

"The entire population of America was aroused to fight when Japan attacked Pearl Harbor while its ambassadors were meeting with our officials in Washington, D.C. It created the racism that still exists in many Americans. For the first time in my life

America was united. Our common goal was to beat the 'Japs' and win a righteous war. Without that attack, I doubt that America would have been united in the fight that has led to a democratic way of life in much of the world."

"I understand that," Yas finally said. "But I often wonder why the people, the Emperor, went along with military rule for so long."

"Did they have a choice, Yas?" I asked. "Or did they even want to choose? After all, the war with America didn't begin with Pearl Harbor. It began with the Japanese invasion of China. Even though many of your military leaders had studied in America, they certainly underestimated the power of the United States. Many of them knew the odds against winning a war with America but did nothing about it. From what I have read, they knew that Japan only had enough fuel and materials to sustain a war for two years, yet they let the rule by committee prevail.

"Can you imagine what Japan might have been today had operation 'Olympic' actually begun? Can you imagine an invasion that might have prolonged the war for years versus the bombs that ended the war in a few days?"

Yas looked at me, shook his head and mumbled, "That would be hard to comprehend."

"Many Japanese leaders were anxious to let the invasion begin," I said, "and then opt for surrender. The bombs killed 178,000. How many more would have died in an invasion? One million? Two million? Three million? It is conceivable that the bombs saved lives and gave the Japanese government an opportunity to save face. It provided an opening for Japan to accept the terms offered by the Americans and preserve a way of life that has existed for centuries and, hopefully, will continue for centuries more. In my mind, the dropping of the bombs in 1945 has prevented their use in all the conflicts the world has seen since. It ended the war. Its effect has acted as a deterrent and, hopefully, it will never be used again."

Yas looked out across the porch to the Pacific Ocean, leaned against the rail, head slightly bowed, and stood there silently for five minutes. I wondered what he was thinking. Did I say something that made him angry?

I went into the kitchen and made some iced tea. When I returned to the porch, Yas looked up at me and in a quiet, pensive voice said, "You are right, Jerry, perhaps this was the best way to end a horrible war. I only wish you could tell this to more of my countrymen. Our understanding of those times is so limited. Our government has never allowed a full disclosure of these events, and now, the younger generation hears little about the war."

"Perhaps I will, Yas."

I put my arm around my friend and led him into the house. I felt relieved. It was as if I had been speaking to a spokesman from Japan rather than to Yas, my friend. As if he answered for the country, not for himself.

"Tough few days, eh, Yas?" I reflected.

"Yes, Jerry San, but worthwhile. I think I understand you and your country a little better, and I hope you can say the same about Japan."

It had been a difficult conversation for both of us. I saw that he felt better, and I did too. What impressed me the most was his ability to accept what I had said. That did not come easy for him.

We enjoyed the rest of the weekend together walking on the beach, talking about general issues, and visiting the golf range. I gave him a putter that he had used when we played at Torrey Pines. He left on an early train from Del Mar on Monday morning. I did not see him again until the day of Robert's wedding.

CHAPTER
FIFTEEN

Robert's Meeting

IN EARLY SEPTEMBER Robert called to tell us he had met with Mr. Yamakawa and two of Takako's brothers.

"Mr. Yamakawa arranged to meet us at a family restaurant for lunch," Robert said. "He and two of his sons were already there when Takako and I arrived. We were served lunch in a private room. It was very cordial and polite. Kiyotaka and Tadashi, Takako's two oldest brothers, asked many questions. Mr. Yamakawa sat silently as I answered them.

'Why do want to marry our sister?'

'Do you intend to remain in Japan?'

'What do you do for a living?'

'Can you support her?' "

"What did you tell them?" I asked. I was anxious to hear Robert's explanation of their meeting, to hear about Mr. Yamakawa.

"I answered them honestly and frankly," Robert said. "I told them that I love Takako, that I see in her the qualities that I admire in a woman. She has a quiet dignity that is appealing to me. I told them that I enjoy her sense of humor, her sense of style; that I am sure that she will be a good wife and an excellent mother for our children."

"Did they accept that?" I asked. "Did they want to know how long you planned to stay in Japan?"

"I told them I did not know how long I would remain in Japan. I really don't have any intention of leaving in the near future.

"You know Dad, I am happy in my work here, and I think I am a making a contribution. I see several hundred people a week in my classes. We talk about current events, about the environment, about Japanese and American customs, and we are constantly learning from each other. I have had some students for several years, and I see progress in them. I don't mean just in their English, but in their attitude. Last year we were talking about Earth Day in America and one of the women asked 'Why don't we have an Earth Day in Mishima?' I thought it would be a good idea, so Richard and I joined with the people in my class, they call themselves, the Global Intercultural Association, and helped organize the first Earth Day in Mishima. I am helping to bridge a gap between what my Japanese students knew about America and Americans. In order for our countries to grow and prosper together, it is necessary for Japanese people to speak and truly understand English. That is what I am trying to accomplish in my work. And I make a good living.

"I think everything went well with my meeting, because during the conversation, Mr. Yamakawa sat silently, listening to what I had to say. When he did start to speak, Dad, he asked about you. His questions were direct and he asked them all at once.

'How old is your father?'

'What does he do?'

'Was he in the war?'

'What branch of service?'

"I could see that he was really interested when I told him you were a pilot in the Air Corps. He asked what airplane you flew. When I said a P-51, he really got excited and asked me where. I said to him, 'All that I know, Mr. Yamakawa, is that my father flew over Japan from Iwo Jima. He escorted B-29s and went on strafing missions. The only detail he ever told me about the war was when I was living in Numazu. He acknowledged that he had strafed Numazu on one of his missions. My father never talked about the war to me.'

"The Yamakawa brothers seemed to accept my answers but then they asked, 'What will you and Takako do if you do not receive our father's permission to get married?' "

"That is something I never considered, Rob, did you?" I asked.

"Takako and I touched on the subject, Dad, but we really never considered that happening."

"What if it does?"

"I'm not sure that I would want to get married and live here without the support of Takako's family. On the other hand, I want to marry Takako, so, if they say no, it will be a real problem for us. Takako has great respect for her family, and I can't imagine her going against their wishes. Let's hope that they say 'yes'."

"When will you know, Rob?" I asked.

"Probably in a few days. They will have to make a decision now that we have met. Mr. Takesue, my go-between, will call the Yamakawas today or tomorrow. That will set well with them because it is their tradition. After that conversation, everyone seemed to relax, the tension went out of the room, and I found out a little about Kiyotaka and Tadashi. Kiyotaka is a bacteriologist and lives in Kanazawa with his wife and two sons. Tadashi is a geologist, married and living in Yokohama. There is one more brother, Masato, an engineer who lives at home. I guess that they will say something to Takako when they make a decision."

"What about Takako, Rob?" I asked. "The last time we saw her she seemed concerned about her family's reaction to you?"

"She has had a rough summer, Dad. She told me she appreciated your openness and acceptance, and she was depressed after you left. Your attitude is so different from her parents. I think she is writing Mom a letter about this whole thing."

Robert told us it was tedious work for Takako to write a letter in English. First, she had to write in Japanese, translate into English and type it on a word processor. Robert then corrected it before Takako retyped it and mailed it to us. Helene received Takako's letter a few weeks after they had met with Mr. Yamakawa. It read.

> I was very happy to meet you and Jerry last March. I am sorry to have taken so much time to write to you and thank you for your encouragement. I wish my parents felt as you do. My mother was against

my involvement with Robert, but I am set on my plans to marry him. I needed time to find the courage to tell my father. My mother is the type of woman who would agree with any decision my father would make, so he is the one I had to convince. But it has taken me much longer than I ever thought it would to speak to him about Robert. Robert is an American who, I thought, couldn't speak Japanese too well. He wore a full, heavy beard. That alone seemed bad enough, but on top of it, his father had actually attacked Japan from the air during the war, even strafing the very town where I had been born. I couldn't see Robert making a good impression. I cried a great deal and became far too upset and afraid to say anything. Instead of acting to clear the air, I just became more and more depressed.

Finally in August, with my friend Kiyo's encouragement, I did speak to my father. I told him I had someone I wanted him to meet.

"I see," said my father. "You must mean that foreigner. Give me some time to think about it."

Days passed with no conversation about our talk. Then, with no warning, my brothers arrived. One came from Kanazawa, seven hours away, and the other from Yokohama, a three-hour journey. The emergency family council took place. I was asked many questions from all sides. What kind of a person is Robert? Why is he in Japan? Does he intend to return to his country soon? What kind of school did he graduate from? What is his religion? And more. Most of the questions were asked by Tadashi and Kiyotaka, my brothers. My father kept his mouth closed and watched the scene out of the corner of his eyes, and just listened. My brothers finally gave their permission to arrange a meeting with Robert.

When the day of the meeting arrived I was apprehensive and nervous. My father had arranged for us to have lunch in a private room at a Japanese family restaurant with a lovely garden. The meeting went much better than I had expected. In fact, now that I think about it, I wonder how my father was able to hold back all the emotion I knew he felt. He always had dreams for his only daughter, and they did not include marrying a foreigner, especially an American, his old enemy!

That night, I sat down with my father and talked with him about the meeting with Robert. He told me, "The day you showed me the picture of all of those foreign men and said you wished to marry one of the men in the picture was a difficult day for me. I knew that some day I would have to let my 'treasured daughter' go, and I knew you were now reaching marriageable age, but I was astonished by the suddenness of the proposition.

"In the picture were several foreign men, but of all the choices, the heavily bearded American one was your choice! Again I was shocked. My feelings towards America and the war were frozen deep within me. I was just beginning, after forty-three years, to accept the changing times. For all those years, I was pretending to be flexible and adaptable. But now you, my daughter, wanted to marry an American, out of all the choices available to you among Japanese men. To marry the son of my enemy!

"I had brought up my children without interfering in their lives. I always believed in the child's independence as much as possible. I only forbid actions that would interfere with others' wellbeing. I encouraged my children to strive for whatever they believed in; but this? It seemed that you had thought through your decision very well. I knew that you had talked to your mother and that she had been quite adamant. 'No *gaijins* in our family,' your mother said.

"If I said no, it would go against my philosophy. Your mother and I put our heads together and finally decided that the least we could do was to meet your young man.

"I was quite surprised to find that Robert was accustomed to the Japanese language, as well as the Japanese lifestyle. Moreover, I found, he was a likable person with a keen interest in *wabi* and *sabi* (the taste for simplicity and tranquility the Japanese consider the ultimate state of being), even beyond the level a Japanese man might show. He also possessed a stillness that has become rather rare in modern-day Japan. I liked him very much. Then, in the ensuing conversation, I learned that his father and I had a lot in common, both in age and in our life experiences. When I heard that Robert's father had been an ace pilot in the war, I had a premonition of the decision that I would make regarding your marriage.

"For myself, even though I sought the path of a pilot in the war, I never realized my dream. But I steadfastly held to the firm belief that there were no enemies in 'the ones who flew in the sky.' Although in the past we were enemies, there is an affinity between all fellow fliers, just from the experience of flying; regardless of being friend or foe.

"Robert also mentioned that his father had flown the P-51 Mustang over Japan. My emotion changed from simple admiration to overwhelming wonder. The P-51 had been the object of adoration of all Japanese student pilots. I imagined that anyone flying that plane would be an extraordinary person, and I was convinced that this young man had, in his blood, much of what I admired. It was all I could handle to keep my composure, suppressing my desire to shout for joy that my only daughter would pick such an excellent counterpart. I did not say anything to you about my thoughts, because I wanted to speak to your mother first. When I told her about my feelings, that I thought your young man was suitable for you to marry, she quickly agreed to my decision. So, Takako, I am very happy for you, and most anxious to meet your new parents."

I cried with joy at what my father told me.

That conversation cleared the air between my mother and me so we began to look for a place to have the wedding reception. We already knew that I would have the ceremony at the Mishima shrine, that is where all of our family occasions are held. We hope to get the Skylight Room at the Mishima Plaza Hotel for the dinner reception after the wedding ceremony. Robert will call you as soon as we have set a firm date.

Signed
Takako Yamakawa

Robert's call came in mid-September.

"The wedding is set for March 5. Is that all right with you? Will you and Mom be able to come?"

"With bells on, Rob, we wouldn't miss it for the world!"

Helene and I wanted to plan a reception for Robert and Takako when they set a date. I asked Robert, "Do you think you and Takako could come here to meet everyone before the wedding?"

"Great idea, let me see if I can work it out. We both get time off in December, maybe we can come then."

Unbelievable! The wedding would take place almost 43 years to the day I went into combat!

The day after Robert's phone call, I wrote a letter to Mr. Yamakawa:

September 22, 1987

My Dear Yamakawa Family:

It is with great pleasure that I send you greetings from America. We were very pleased when Robert phoned us last night and informed us of his plans to marry Takako in March of next year. We think it is exciting for them. You can be assured that Takako will be welcomed into our family by Robert's brothers and my wife and me, with love and respect.

We were told by Takako in April that you Yamakawa-San, and I share a lot in common. It seems we were born in the same month of the same year, shared similar experiences in our youth, and then devoted the rest of our lives to what we felt was most important of all, raising our families. Both of us have four children, all of whom have good education and futures. You and I have strong marriages, and now, these two families will be joined together by the marriage of our youngest children.

I can fully understand that you might be upset by Takako's decision to marry a man other than a Japanese because of the difference in tradition and culture. We, too, had some doubts as to the wisdom of this decision. However, the more we examined your traditions and culture, we saw that there were many more similarities than differences. Truly what matters to us is the respect that two people have for each other and the fact that they want to be with each other as a family, much as we have led our lives.

We want you to know that we are all happy for Takako and Robert and we wish them a long and happy life together.

We look forward with great enthusiasm to meeting you and your family in February and being part of the wedding on March 5th.

Signed,

Jerry and Helene Yellin

In a few weeks Mr. Yamakawa responded. His letter was in the form of a beautiful, ancient scroll and, of course, in Japanese. Thoughtfully, they had included a translation which read:

Dear Mr. and Mrs. Yellin:

Here the season of autumn is beginning to appear in the trees and in the air. It seems that fate has brought your warm letter to us from so far away. We are grateful that Takako is welcomed into Robert's family with such a warm feeling. We would like to thank your family.

When Takako told us of Robert and their plans it was like a bolt out of the blue. But after we met Robert and saw his quietness and consideration, we found that our daughter's eyes were correct. After Robert told us about his father, it seems we are of the same age and shared similar backgrounds. We feel happy to see your pictures and know that Takako will be accepted into such a good and healthy family.

Although our customs and lifestyles are different, in these modern times, they may be interchangeable. I expect that Robert and Takako will be able to do this. Our family is not so well off, but our hearts and feelings are like the sky. We always want to have that feeling, plentiful, and wide like the blue sky. Our distance is far but we are happy to be family and relatives, distance cannot change these situations. We are very happy.

March 5th is a lucky day for marriage at the Mishima Shrine. It will soon be here. At that time you will be here, we look forward to that day and are glad to think of it now. We answer your letter in happiness and wish you health and happiness in your life and work.

Signed,

Taro and Hatsue Yamakawa.

When I received his letter I felt compelled to reply.

October 24th, 1987

Dear Yamakawa-San:

I am writing to you today with a wonderful feeling of happiness, respect and gratefulness to you and your family. Your letter expressed, in poetic terms, a beautiful sentiment that could only come from a man of depth and great understanding. Both Helene and I are deeply touched by your words and your thoughts.

Even more, it has given us an insight into Takako's background and upbringing and strengthened our feelings about the coming wedding. Only you and I, Yamakawa-San, can know about the soul-searching we both had to go through to reach this level of complete acceptance. We are soon to be family and share in the joys of that which families experience. This is all the wealth that I believe a man needs. We indeed are both fortunate to have reached this stage of life.

We will be arriving in Japan on Saturday, February 27 and plan to stay two weeks. We look forward to meeting you and your family and spending time getting to know you.

Please give my warmest regards to your wife, your sons, and my future daughter.

Signed,

Jerry Yellin

And so my enemy became my friend. I felt his warmth across the ocean and he felt mine.

CHAPTER SIXTEEN

The Wedding

CHAPTER
SIXTEEN

Fly Weighing

WE HAD AN engagement party for Robert and Takako in San Diego on December 28th. It was Takako's first trip on an airplane, her first time out of Japan. She was very excited about being in America, meeting Robert's brothers and their wives, and seeing us again. We, in turn, were happy to have her with us.

This was the first time our entire family had been together for a long time. Robert had not been in the States for several years, and he enjoyed catching up with all of the events in his brother's lives. They, in turn, were extremely happy to meet Takako.

The party was a huge success. We invited Robert's friends from college and most of them came. We were all impressed with Takako's ability to communicate in English, her charming manner, and delightful, childlike awe of much of what she saw in San Diego. Helene and I were delighted when we saw Patti and Gail, David's and Michael's wives, talking animatedly with Takako. These were our three daughters-in-law and we wanted them to be close. Shortly after the wedding, Patti and David visited Robert and Takako in Japan. A short time later, Michael and Gail went for a visit too.

Takako was most impressed with our supermarkets. "I can't believe how big they are, how much food there is in them," she exclaimed. "We have everything you have but not in so much volume."

"In Japan," Robert explained, "Takako shops almost every day for her needs. Partly because she likes to have fresh food and partly because the storage area in the refrigerator is so small. She buys a few stalks of celery instead of the whole bunch, a few strawberries, rather than a basket. That is the way those items are packaged in Japan."

Takako and Robert remained in San Diego for a couple of days after the party, then went to Los Angeles for two days of sight-seeing before returning to Japan.

The trip to Japan for Robert and Takako's wedding was our third on Singapore Airlines from Los Angeles. I was familiar with the seating in business class and arranged for seats on the upper deck of the 747. The airport at Narita was familiar this time and we knew exactly what to do after we gathered our luggage. Neither Helene nor I wanted to make the four-hour trip to Mishima after the long flight from California, so we checked into a motel in the nearby town. It was only seven-thirty in the evening when we retired and four in the morning when we awakened. By six we were ready for the one hour bus ride to the Tokyo train station where we had breakfast and caught a nine o'clock train to Mishima.

Shortly before we arrived at each station, chimes

sounded and a soft, gentle, feminine voice announced in English, "we will soon be arriving for a brief stop in Atami, (or Mishima). The exit will be on the left, or right side."

Robert was standing at the foot of the stairs of the platform when the train pulled into the station promptly at ten o'clock.

We met the Yamakawas a few days before the wedding: Helene, Robert, Takako, her mother and father, and me. It was awkward because of our language difference but not at all strained by the circumstance. I had felt apprehensive before we left for the restaurant. This was to be my first encounter with a Japanese man who was my own age and who had fought in the war. We arrived almost at the same time, so our introductions took place in the parking lot. Mr. Yamakawa and I were both carrying shopping bags with presents. When Robert made the introductions, we put the bags down and shook hands warmly. Both of us had wide grins on our faces and, at that moment, a bond seemed to form between us. I felt the tension leave me.

We sat down for dinner together in a Chinese restaurant. We ate, chatted about our families, exchanged gifts, looked at each other with understanding and affection, and smiled a lot. We gave Mrs. Yamakawa a box containing our gift. She immediately put it aside. I looked at Helene and asked, "Isn't she going to open it?" Robert then told us that it was not the custom to open presents in front of the giver, "Sort of prevents any embarrassment," he said.

We really wanted them to open the presents and

suggested that we should do it the American way and open them now. The Yamakawas laughed when Robert translated our request, and Mrs. Yamakawa carefully opened the box, using a toothpick so as not to tear the paper. We had given her a gold butterfly pin on a chain that had belonged to my mother. She put it on immediately and remarked, "I have never had such a beautiful piece of jewelry." We had a Cross pen and pencil set for Mr. Yamakawa.

We knew it was customary to exchange gifts in Japan, but it is always difficult to decide what to bring from America. Something small and easy to pack, something of quality but not too expensive. Helene gave Takako a pair of antique bracelets that I had given to her many years ago. All of the gifts were received graciously. Mr. and Mrs. Yamakawa gave Helene a beautiful silk scarf, and I received a Minolta camera complete with an extra lens, flash attachment, film and carrying case. It was a genuine show of affection and acceptance of our children's decision to join the two families together. The evening passed quickly and we departed feeling that the Yamakawas were genuine friends.

But I wanted more, I wanted to talk about the war, to find out about Mr. Yamakawa's involvement. I wanted to share my experiences with him and have him tell me about his. After all that we had both been through, how could we accept each other's children into our families without knowing something about each other's wartime experiences? I wanted to get to know this man who would also be the grandfather of my grandchildren. His background, his feelings about life, were important to me. One of my sons was about to become one of his sons.

Before leaving I asked Takako to find out when her father and I could spend some time together, alone with an interpreter. A day later she told me that her father would make arrangements for us to spend some time together at a *ryokan* a few days after the wedding. He requested that I ask Mr. Osada, Robert's friend, to be the interpreter.

As I dressed, on the morning of the wedding, I thought about the war, about people, about the guys I knew who had died hating the Japanese. I thought about the pleasures of life that I had and they did not. I thought about the wonders of the intimate relationship I had with Helene, of raising a family, of seeing and feeling and experiencing the joy of accomplishment. Of having the gift of life. Of growing old. I thought about other wars in other times. Of my scrapbook, my medals, my wings, and my pictures that were now in the museum.

From my recent experiences with the Japanese people, from the love I had developed for the country, its customs and people, from recognizing all war as obscenity, I was now totally prepared to accept Robert's path in life. Yas had briefed me about some of the intricacies and deeply significant aspects of marriage in Japan. I reminded myself that, to the Japanese, a wedding is the joining of families as well as individuals.

The wedding of our son Robert to Takako Yamakawa took place on March 5, 1988, (a lucky day

for marriage, called *taian* in Japanese) at the Mishima
Shrine.

The Plaza Hotel, adjacent to the Shrine in
Mishima, is similar to a wedding hall in the States.
Seven wedding ceremonies were scheduled for March
5th, and timetables were set and rigidly adhered to.
Takako was to begin her preparations at 10 A.M,
Robert at 11 A.M., and the family would meet at noon.

It took three attendants two hours to dress
Takako in a traditional wedding kimono, apply white
make-up to her face, and arrange her hair and wig.
Takako described her ordeal to us later in the week.

"On the day of the wedding," she told us, "I
arrived at the Mishima Plaza Hotel three hours prior
to the ceremony. I went immediately to the beauty
parlor to have my face made up. Unlike my natural
skin color, my face was made completely white. Even
the nape of my neck and my arms, up to my elbows,
anywhere that the kimono would not cover, was painted white. Next, they fitted the wig I had chosen on to
my head. I put on ceremonial combs and other hair
ornaments, and finally, my lipstick. I was then finished
with that portion of the dressing. It had taken an hour.
When I looked at myself in the mirror I laughed. My
face looked like a woman from an historical drama,
but I was wearing western clothing, jeans and a tee
shirt. It was difficult to walk at first. The wig is heavy,
about twenty pounds, and my center of gravity
seemed to have shifted. It took several minutes to
become accustomed to the weight.

"In an adjoining dressing room, I put on my
kimono with the help of two attendants. There are

several 'under kimonos' and sashes that have to be put on first. The outer garment, the colorful, red and gold brocaded kimono that I had selected with my parents help, came next. In Japanese it is called *Irouchkake*. These kimonos are extremely expensive, and since they are only worn once, they are rented. Mine cost $4000 for the day. Half of that money goes toward the cleaning and packing of the kimono after the wedding is over."

Robert was helped to dress in his wedding kimono by Mr. Yamakawa. Before the ceremony, the bride and groom spend thirty minutes posing for formal wedding pictures. This was the first time that I had seen Robert in traditional Japanese clothing, (*Haori* and *hakama*, a skirted bottom and coat-like top). I was concerned about how he would look and was pleasantly surprised how natural and handsome he was. The weather was quite cold for early March, and Robert wore silk long johns to keep warm in the unheated rooms and shrine."

At the appointed hour of noon, Robert and Takako walked to the special room set aside for the Yellin/Yamakawa wedding party. We joined them there to meet the entire Yamakawa family and the rest of the wedding party. This wedding was scheduled for one o'clock, so we only had to wait about twenty minutes before we had to leave for the Mishima Taisha.

I gasped audibly as Helene and I walked into the room and saw Robert and Takako dressed for their wedding. The bride was wearing a traditional head-dress and wig; her face was masked in white make-up and she was wearing an exquisite red and gold kimono. She was sitting on a small stool surrounded by attendants. Robert looked handsome dressed in a Japanese wedding robe. The women were all dressed in black kimonos trimmed with gold; the men, in dark suits with white ties. It looked like a play, or a movie, a scene I could only comprehend from afar.

At precisely 12:20 P.M. the entire entourage, including Takako's family, the Master of Ceremonies, the go-between, and Obaasan (Robert's Japanese grandmother) were escorted to the ground floor of the hotel. Takako, Robert, and the attendants were seated in a vintage Rolls Royce for the ride to the temple. Taro, Helene, and I decided to walk to the shrine. Hatsue and the other members of the family rode in mini-vans. As the Rolls drove by, I noticed people smiling and waving. Helene and I were very proud.

We entered the approach to the temple, crossed a stone bridge over a pond filled with Koi, and waited for Robert and Takako to make their appearance. When the family had gathered, we entered the temple grounds through huge, carved wooden doors and walked to a small building. After removing our shoes, we were escorted into a large *tatami* room where, I was told, the families would be formally introduced. For generation in Japan, weddings were arranged and the families often did not actually meet until the day of the wedding. This was often true of the bride and groom as well. That custom has changed over the years, but the tradition of formal introductions of family is still adhered to, and a formal introduction is always planned. Takako and Robert sat on small stools facing the door as we walked into the long, narrow, matted room. Square cushions were set on the floor about four feet apart.

We were directed to specific places, where we knelt barefoot on the cushions while two Shinto "virgin girl" attendants rehearsed Robert and Takako in the proper technique of holding and using their fans. Later, in the ceremony, tree branches were substituted for the fans.

We were served a special wedding tea, made of seaweed. When we were all seated, and the teacups removed, we were each introduced, one by one, by Mr. Takesue. He gave a brief history of everyone in attendance and their relationship. After each person was introduced, they bowed almost to the floor from their kneeling position. It was very moving to be part of this ancient custom. Now, no longer strangers, all would be recognized as family from this day forward. No words were exchanged and, when the last introduction was over, we were escorted by the attendants, in specific order, to the temple itself.

Few get a chance to enter the temple. Prayers are said from the outside looking in. Again we were seated in a precise order. Robert and Takako sat facing the stage, the bride's family on their left facing them, and the groom's family on their right, also facing them.

At precisely 1:00 P.M. a Shinto Priest started the ceremony by vigorously beating a large, bass drum. The deep sound reverberated throughout the wooden structure. As the drum sound faded, flutists began a haunting, mystical song, and the elder priest began a chant. The girl attendants danced slowly to the rhythm of the flutes. Robert and Takako rose and walked forward. The Shinto priest performed a purification rite on Robert and Takako; he offered salt and rice at the altar and then recited a Shinto prayer to the gods.

Next came *sankon no qui*, generally known as *san san kudo*. This is the act of drinking sacred *sake*, poured by *miko*, the virgin-girl assistants. The first cup is drunk by the groom, the second by the bride, and the third again by the groom, using three different sized *sake* cups. Robert then read from a scroll in Japanese, a chance for him to display his proficiency with the language. Mr. Takesue, Robert's go-between, accompanied him to the altar and assisted him with the unfamiliar words. The pledge Robert read vowed, in front of the gods, his intention of marriage. Finally, the two of them offered the *Tamagu shi*, the blessing using a branch of the *sakaki* tree with white prayer papers attached. While this was happening, all the relatives received a cup of *sake*, which we drank together in three sips. This is called *Katame* and signifies that the bride and groom and their families have become united as one.

After the ceremony Robert and Takako, now man and wife, and the rest of the wedding party, walked out of the temple together. There, in the courtyard, a photographer was waiting to take an official family picture. This complete, we all walked to the waiting transportation back to the Mishima Plaza Hotel. As Robert and Takako walked together, they were greeted with applause by people in the area. Many surprised onlookers shouted "*Gaijin! Gaijin!*" and grinned.

At the reception afterwards, Yas Takesue began the proceedings. When the guests were seated, Robert and Takako walked into the hall and stood beside Yas on the dais. As Robert's go-between, Yas, the only person in attendance who knew about our entire family, began a lengthy introduction of the Yellins. I recognized several words he had to say in English, like P-51, and looked around to see if there was any reaction. Obviously, he was talking about my war experiences. Then he spoke about Helene and our sons, David, Steven, Michael, and, finally, Robert. It was a long speech, more than fifteen minutes, and I could see Takako's head rolling slightly from the weight of her headdress. Yas then introduced Mr. Osada, the Master of Ceremonies, who also made a speech about his friendship with Robert.

One of Robert's young students sat at our table to translate the speeches for us. Unfortunately, she was so engrossed in the subject matter, that she did not tell us very much. When the ceremony was finally over, Mr. Takesue gave us a run down of what was said. Mr. Osada called on Mr. Yamamoto, Robert's first host in Japan and the head of the honored family. Both Takuya and Koji, their two sons, were at the wedding. Erina was forbidden to come by her mother. She had an important high school entrance exam in a few days and had to stay home to study.

Mr. Yamamoto spoke about the impact Robert had on their lives while he lived with them for two years. He remarked, "How fortunate we were to have selected him in the lottery held for the American students in 1983. Now, five years later, my adopted son is getting married. My family will never be the same because of the wonderful influence Robert brought into our home. My daughter has been to America, my sons have learned that all people are the same, and my wife and I have improved our English."

He then called on his mother, Robert's Japanese grandmother, to come to the microphone to sing a song. Obaasan, stooped and small but lively, walked to the front of the room, and in a strong, melodic, voice sang an ancient wedding blessing. Her gaze never wavered from Robert and Takako. All of us were moved by this beautiful rendition by the elderly grandmother.

I don't think Takako could have stood there much longer. Finally, after the formalities, the bride and groom broke a large wooden cask of *sake*, a ceremony similar to the cutting of a cake. The *sake* was served amid a rousing cheer of *kampai!*, and Robert and Takako left to change their clothes. When they returned, he was wearing a tuxedo and she a beautiful, red, hooped gown. Robert's good friend, Richard, referred to it as a "Gone With the Wind" gown, as it reminded him of a southern belle he had seen in the film. Later, more *sake* was served in wooden cups. During the feast, the bride and groom went to the tables and signed each attendee's cup.

Japanese weddings are about speeches. The Master of Ceremonies has a schedule, and he also can call upon anyone, at any time, to talk, sing, or dance. After speeches by some of Robert's and Takako's friends and Takako's *kendo* teacher, a wartime friend of

Mr. Yamakawa's was so moved that he stopped the proceedings and asked to speak.

"I must speak today," he said. "I have carried the burden of the war for forty-three years, without ever revealing my feelings to anyone. Now, I must reveal those dreadful thoughts that I have lived with for so long. I was always proud of our service in the Imperial Army. When I left for China, I was looking forward to doing my part for the Emperor, my country, and the greater Asian Co-Prosperity Sphere. We were on a divine mission. At that age, nineteen, we were embarking on the greatest adventure any man could ever hope for. To fight, and maybe die, for one's country would have been the greatest honor. When I returned from overseas, I was deeply moved by what I saw. Our towns had been destroyed, there was no trace of the school I had attended, and I learned that only eight of us were left from our graduation class. For all these years I have carried a deep feeling of sorrow and shame. Not for the humiliation of defeat, but for the havoc we allowed to happen to our country. I have never been able to say these things, but today I feel relieved of hatred I have felt for Americans, for the damage that they did to our country and way of life.

"I realized only after I saw Robert and Takako standing in front of me, as man and wife, that I was responsible for those deep feelings of hatred. I feel that a weight of great magnitude has been lifted from my shoulders. I am glad to be a part of the joining of my friend's daughter to the son of our enemy. And I drink a toast of good health to all of you here."

His speech moved everyone, and when I heard the translation I had no control of my emotions, my eyes filled with tears.

At 4:30 P.M. the room was darkened and spotlights shone on Helene and me and on the Yamakawas, as Robert presented a huge bouquet to his new mother and father. Takako did the same for us. At that point, I was called upon to speak.

I spoke about war and weddings. I spoke of our initial uncertainty about the marriage; about our pleasure at its consolidation. Toward the end I found myself referring to Taro Yamakawa.

"We have grown from enemy, to friend, and now to family. And that is as it should be. Now, a new generation will be started by Robert and Takako; a generation that will not be bound by rigid constraints imposed by cultural or national boundaries. We wish them a long, productive, fruitful life together; incorporating the best of each of their backgrounds into the next generation, and the creation of a peaceful world of their future."

The wedding was over, but not the party. Helene and I drove with the Yamakawas to a *ryokan* about thirty minutes away. When we arrived, the men and women of each family separated and took long, talkative baths together, as is the tradition. Then we all assembled in a large room and ate a traditional wedding feast as a family.

The next morning Takako told me her father would like to speak to me about the war before I returned home. "My father has arranged a three-day trip down the Izu Peninsula for all of us. We will stay at a different *ryokan* each night. Since he has to work each day, he can not drive with us, but he will meet us each evening. Mr. Osada has agreed to drive with us and act as the interpreter. I will stay with you for the entire time, but Robert will have to return to Mishima after the first day to teach. We will spend the last evening in Shimoda, at the tip of the Izu Peninsula. Is that all right with you?"

I was overwhelmed. Taro wanted us to have a good time, to spend a few nights in splendid surroundings, to feel Japan. *Ryokan* are very expensive, upward of $150 a night per person. When I offered to pay, Taro refused to accept any money from me. Incredible, I thought, such hospitality, and on our son's honeymoon, as well.

We began our short trip a day after the wedding. We drove down the peninsula, stopping every now and again to view the splendid sight of Mt. Fuji from different view points. The roads were steep and curved sharply around the mountains. Some were completely covered with cherry tree branches just beginning to blossom. The scenery was spectacular. We stopped the first night half way down the peninsula at an ancient inn. After an afternoon bath, we dined on wild boar and pheasant, both indigenous to the area. After dinner we watched, then participated in, a rice pounding ceremony in the lobby of the inn. Each of us took turns swinging a large mallet at rice in the carved out hollow of a tree stump until the rice thickened and could be rolled into cookies. The cookies were called sticky rice balls. I didn't like the taste of them, even though they were considered a delicacy. Taro and I took a short walk along a fast moving stream before we retired for the night. All was quite natural even though we could not talk to each other.

The next morning we began the drive to Shimoda, arriving shortly before noon. Taro had arranged for the son of the owner of Seriyu-so, the inn at which we were staying, to drive us around the area and take us to lunch. Helene and I rode in the back seat of a large Volvo, listening to Bach on the stereo system, enjoying the beautiful seascapes of the south-ern-most tip of the Izu Peninsula. Bach, we were told, is the favorite composer of many Japanese. "We admire the orderliness of his sounds," they stated.

The rocky coast, pine trees bending to the wind and the crashing surf reminded us of the Big Sur area of northern California. For lunch we were taken to a restaurant that served only eels. The only disagreeable aspect of the entire trip was walking past large baskets of eels as we climbed the stairs of the restaurant to our private dining area. Eating them after seeing them took away some of the pleasure of the lunch.

As we were dining, I reflected that Admiral Perry first landed at Shimoda. It was there that the first American envoy to Japan lived. After lunch, we were driven to the home of the driver's grandmother, a large, thatched-roof house in the center of town. It was over four hundred years old, we were told, and has been handed down from generation to generation. "My father owns it now," the driver said, "and I, as the oldest son, will inherit it next."

We had tea and sweets with his grandmother,

were given a tour of the house and, at four, we returned to Seriyu-so. Helene and I were staying in the same suite that Jimmy Carter and his wife occupied during a state visit when he was President. Takako, Taro, and Mr. Osada shared a large room on the second floor of our suite. Helene and Takako left together for the bath area after we agreed to meet for dinner at seven. Taro, Mr. Osada, and I went to the men's bathing area to begin our talk. I wanted to hear about Taro's experiences in the war, how he felt about Americans, and how he felt about Robert, in particular. I wanted him to know about my experiences first hand, and how I felt about our children's marriage.

We sat and soaked in the hot water, discussing our feelings about life, and the excitement and happiness we were experiencing at our children's marriage. I started to talk first. "When we met Takako," I began, "our only concern was, 'How would Robert be accepted by her family?' It was in you, Yamakawa San [Taro], that I had the most interest when we first met our future daughter. What did you do in the war? Did you feel about America and Americans as I felt about Japan and the Japanese? Could you accept a son into your family whose father flew over your country as a fighter pilot?

"So I wrote you a letter about how we felt. Your response was more than I could have hoped for, and it brought tears into my eyes when I read it. I told Helene that when we met, I was going to take you into my arms and hug you. She laughed and said, 'That isn't done,' but it did not change my feelings about what I wanted to do."

I spoke about flying over Japan, about dog fighting, the dangers of strafing, about losing so many
friends, and the hatred that I carried in my heart for
so many years. When he asked what it was like to fly
in combat, I told him it was exhilarating. I said I
enjoyed feeling a part of the war against my hated
enemy.

"You are the first Japanese man who served in the
military that I have ever spoken to about the war. I feel
lightened of the terrible burden that I have carried
these many years.

"I see in you and your family what I see in mine.
In your children, I see four fine, caring people. I see in
you and Hatsue the same loving, respectful relationship that Helene and I have. I feel in Japan a stillness
and beauty that I have experienced in the woods and
mountains of America.

"We know the truth, Yamakawa San. War is a terrible thing. I hope that our grandchildren will not
have to experience what we did when we were young
men.

"This is a very beautiful moment for me. I truly
believe that our children will have a wonderful life
together. When we leave Japan in a few days, we will,
of course, be sad to leave Robert and Takako behind.
But we will leave knowing that he is a part of your
family, and we will not leave with a heavy heart."

I could see that Mr. Yamakawa and Mr. Osada,
the interpreter, were moved by my words.

The small bath area was becoming more crowded, so the three of us walked a few yards to the larger
bath and sat in a corner, facing a wall of windows. The

day was overcast, and the sun was setting behind the clouds. As Mr. Yamakawa started to speak, a ray of sun shone brightly through the clouds on the three of us.

He began slowly. "Jerry San, you have shared much with me, and I am moved to tell you something of my own life."

I saw that it was not easy for him to speak in such an intimate, personal way. It was only a few days after the wedding of his beloved daughter and he was quite emotional.

"You are the first westerner that I have ever spent any time with, Jerry San. Frankly, I am astonished that you feel about your life and your family the same way that I feel about mine.

"Like you, I was concerned about my daughter marrying a non-Japanese man. Especially an American. Although I did not see any personal combat, most of my friends did. Most were killed. I wanted desperately to fire a gun at my enemy, to kill at least one before I gave my life to our Emperor.

"My greatest fear was that my daughter would leave Japan and we would never see her again. I also did not know if she would be accepted into your family.

"Although your letter was important and deeply moving, I did not sleep for three nights, thinking about my youth and the hatred I felt for America. It was not until I met you, saw the kindness and gentility on your face, that I lost my concerns.

"I have felt shame all of my adult life, because I did not fire one shot at my enemy, or complete my flight training, or die for my country and my

Emperor. It was always difficult for me to accept living when so many of my friends and family had died a glorious death.

"But now, today, I am glad that I have lived.

"I see that we are no different from other people. What we were taught in our youth: that we are better, smarter, more industrious than others; that we must never bring shame on our family or country, all this creates a barrier between people. Now that I have met you and Helene, now that I know Robert will not take Takako away, now that I know that we are all the same, that barrier has been lifted.

"Today is a day that I will never forget as long as I live. I am ashamed that I have carried so many negative thoughts about non-Japanese people all of these years.

"When the day finally arrived that we would meet Robert's parents, only three days before the wedding, I was trembling from the tension and excitement. When we met, I saw in you a gentleman, energetic, respectable in appearance, and, in your well-aged state, the self-possessed calmness and passion of pilots. You acted as if we were age-old friends and the tension went away. It was an impressive and touching encounter. Your wife, Helene, is a neat and beautiful woman of virtue. Her actions remind me of the Japanese women of our generation. There was not a moment of that feared sense of unpleasantness.

"On the day of the wedding, the religious ceremony at the Mishima Taisha, was impressive. But your speech was, for me, the climax of the event. I cannot forget the friendship of Mr. Osada, who translated each word with careful interpretation. I felt a feeling of genuine peace come over me, and I was finally able to bid farewell to my heavy and depressing memories of the war. They had haunted me for a long time, and now, they were gone.

"Even though you and I lived during the same period of time, even though we were from hostile countries, I know that there is no difference between human beings. I know that the lives of those from opposing nations would be splendid if only they could meet and touch each other. Now, in my life, I have experienced a great joy through my blood and kin. I really can appreciate the importance of world peace, and the true meaning of internationalization that once I could only capture through concept and theory."

CHAPTER SEVENTEEN

The Fathers

IT WAS IN SHIMODA that Taro Yamakawa and I became more than casual friends; we truly became family. In the ensuing years we have spent many hours together. Our conversations are limited, neither of us can speak the other's language. But the feeling of family and deep friendship prevails. Whenever we are together we manage to laugh with our children who act as our interpreters and enjoy the walks we take on the beach at Hara.

Through the years I had asked him to write his memoirs so I could include them in this story. Taro, like me, never told his children about his war experiences. It took two years of coaxing to get him to put his story on paper. What follows is a literal translation of Taro's biography.

I have lived my entire life in Hara, a town of Numazu in Shizuoka Ken, next to Suruga Bay, in the foothills of Mount Fuji, adjoining the sea. My name, Yamakawa, means mountain river, and I have lived to the rhythm of the sea and the beauty of the mountain all of my life. There exists within me a great satisfaction knowing that I have followed the principles and ways of life of generations of my countrymen. Only twice has my life been disrupted. Once when the great war came, and once when my beloved daughter told me she was going to marry a *gaijin*, a foreigner.

It is said that what we accomplish in life we owe to our blood and to the process of growing up. I was born in the sixth year of the Showa regime on December 6, 1924 in Tokyo. My father, Yamakawa Hidenobu, and my mother, Nakamura Shimo, delayed registering my birth until January 6, 1925, as they thought it best that I should not lose an entire year for the sake of a few days.

January 15th is Genpuku, or Adult's Day, the day all youths of twenty years come of age. From that day forward they will be looked upon as men, and be responsible for all their actions. In the days of the Samurai, the age was fifteen.

We were a family of four until my elder sister passed away in September of that year, at the age of four. My father was a graduate engineer, a rarity in those days, who spoke English quite well and worked for a foreign trading company. In 1927 he became ill with pulmonary tuberculosis and died on March 16, at the age of thirty-three. My own daughter, Takako, was born on that same date in 1964; reminding me of all those years that I did not know the touch of my father.

My mother, at the age of twenty, left with a young son and the memories of her husband and daughter, returned with me to her family home in Niigata, on the Sea of Japan. By custom, a girl, once married, belongs to the family of the husband. Negotiations were held between the families, and a separation was agreed to that took me away from my mother's breast forever. It was decided by the family that it would be best for me to live with my father's family, the Yamakawas.

I was raised by my grandmother and my aunt, descendants of the samurai family Mito. They subsisted on the income from a small pension left by my grandfather, a former stationmaster of the Japanese National Railway, and the earnings of my aunt, a schoolteacher. On their small income it was very difficult keeping up the appearances befitting an ex-stationmaster's family. At the time I was unaware of the difficulties and did not think about it until much later on.

I entered the local Hara Primary School in 1931, graduated in 1937, and enrolled in the Junior High School in Numazu in April of 1937. I was fortunate to have been able to continue my education under the circumstances. As I grew older I realized the strain I placed on the family's finances and, at the age of fifteen, I tried to enlist in the navy. My Uncle Nubuo, my father's younger brother, heard about my plans and stopped me before I left school. He urged me to put all of my efforts into studying, and for that I am grateful.

There was a deeper reason for my wanting to join the navy. From the time of my first memories, perhaps as young as five, when I saw the Koinobori (the huge cloth carp symbolizing "Boys' Day") flying in the sky above the tea fields surrounding my house, I yearned to fly. As I grew older, and played on the beach, I could see and hear the mail plane fly over, and the desire to become a pilot obsessed me. I had reached the age of acceptance in 1940 and the navy flying program was available to all who could pass the exams, regardless of education.

In 1940 the battle front in China expanded. The situation between the United States and Japan became more critical, and our educational system became more war-oriented. We all worked as laborers towards the war effort and participated in long hours of military drill as part of our school day. The public spirit of the entire country was appealed to, and the hot blood surged through our bodies to serve our country. I dreamed of the day I could realize my destiny and achieve immortality as a soldier fighting for his glorious country. In 1941, I took the entrance exam for the naval and military academies.

The naval examination took three days. The first and second days were made up of written examinations. Those not passing were eliminated daily. The third day we had interviews and were measured for uniforms. I reached that third evening hopeful and excited, but I did not receive a letter of acceptance. One of my friends, the brightest student in our entire class, also failed the examination. I heard he was found unsuitable as a naval officer because of his father's position in life. Since I had no father, I could not reflect well on the Academy.

In December 1941, immediately after the Pearl Harbor assault, I took an entrance examination for the naval aviation preparatory course. The tests were rather simple: written in the morning, followed by an interview in the afternoon. Even though I was only in Junior High School, I wanted to serve my country. I was told that I had a 10, a perfect score, in the written exam and a 9 in the physical, and would do well in the program. I waited for word of my acceptance, but none came. I finally asked the Prefecture Officer why I was not accepted. He told me that they could not take me without the consent of my family and, besides, "Who would take care of the elderly women you live with if you were not there?"

Had I been accepted I would have gone through the same training as Jerry San. I would have realized my dream to fly a Zero-Sen (Zero), and, more than likely, I would not have lived to see this day. In my heart I still cannot bear to think that I have lived while so many of my friends and countrymen died an honorable death serving their country.

Ninety per cent of my classmates from Junior High School wished to enter High School. But I wanted to be a part of the war effort so, in January of 1942, I took a job as a clerk in the local National Electric Company. Many of my friends called me a quitter for not continuing my education. But they did not know how much I wanted to fly for my country, or my circumstances at home. I was granted a wartime special exception to leave school and work. My grandmother, who was worried about my strong desire to become a soldier, was delighted with my employment. I worked hard, even giving up my two days off a month. I remember vividly the day my class graduated from Junior High School: March 1, 1942. I received special permission to leave the factory, change into my school uniform, and attend the graduation ceremonies to receive my graduation certificate.

While my friends pursued their education, I worked alongside many other young men of my own age, producing needed war materials. Then, not being satisfied with my lowly existence started to bother me. I thought it would be desirable to acquire some sort of skill, but I did not have any money. Even though I had wanted to work my way through school, it was simply not allowable when the livelihood of my family depended on my earnings. After considerable days of agony, the thought of taking some kind of exam to test my ability came to me, and I decided to aim for Tokyo and the Industrial Chemical Technician training department. Thanks to the kindness and generosity of my employers, I was given a leave of absence, with reduced pay, to study in Tokyo.

I moved in with my uncle in April 1943. I enjoyed the studying but found it hard to cope with the food shortage. Everything was rationed, and my uncle could not provide enough food for his family and for me. I found a restaurant near my factory, and I went there every day to stand in line for *udon* (noodles). It was always crowded, and I had to get in line before eleven in the morning or they would run out of food. Each day I had to ask a colleague to take over the lab test so that I could sneak out.

The newspapers reported the death of our leader Admiral Yamamoto, the evacuation of Guadalcanal, the honorable defeat at Attu, and the battles for the islands of Makin and Tarawa. The excitement of the war was building in me, and I had to find a way to get involved. The draft age had been lowered by one year, and all last-year junior high school students were being drafted. As a Japanese man I felt a strong obligation to my company and what it had done for me and my family. I also understood my loyalty to our emperor and of my love for my country. I was torn between these conflicts and finally decided that my long cherished desire to fulfill my destiny of service to my country and all of my countrymen was more important than any other consideration.

Without consulting anyone, in March of 1944 I enlisted as an Army Special Military Cadet. I had a month before I was called to duty as an aviation cadet. I told my company after I was accepted, and convinced my grandmother that I was about to be drafted in a short time, and anyway I wanted to fly. She reluctantly stood by my decision.

In April I entered the Tachiarai Army Aviation School. I loved every minute of the training, ground school, radio courses, and of the work on the airplanes. Every minute was taken up. We flew gliders, and had war-song singing training, in which we sang to the setting red sun every night. It was a glorious time for me. I was realizing my dream of learning to fly and serving my country. It was here at Tachiarai that I left my teen years behind me.

I had eight hours of flight time in our BU131B, a 105hp, 4-cylinder training plane, when my class was ordered to report to the Third Air Force in Singapore.

We departed from the port of Moji on December

31, 1944 in a large convoy bound for China. It was the last large fleet to leave Japan for the South. I felt the sorrow of parting as I watched the lights of the port grow smaller and smaller, to finally disappear in the distance. We had no idea of our fleet's formation or route.

The trip was difficult. The large seas made most of our group too ill to eat. Fortunately I did not become seasick and so enjoyed filling myself at the two servings we received daily. Our only exercise was occasional emergency evacuation drill. Our ship was a typical freight vessel. We lived in tight quarters, on three-tiered bunks. Mine was on the top, and I spent many hours, while lying there, dreaming of my future.

The ocean was constantly rough, causing the big ship to roll and pitch. The color of the water was brownish-red and turbid; in many ways it made me think of the River Kóga. I got a frightening view of the water every time I went to the toilet. Actually, going to the toilet was very dangerous: two boards were attached to the port side of the ship, extending far out over the side. Twenty meters below were the boiling waves. Keeping your balance while standing, or squatting, was a difficult, serious endeavor!

We knew we were approaching warmer climates when the condensation started dripping from the ceiling of our quarters. I found out later that we had sailed across the Sea of Genkai and then south along the shores of Korea and China to Yangchou. From there we sailed through the channel of Taiwan. On the morning of January 19 we were attacked by enemy submarines. Our ship took evasive action, and the torpedoes missed us, but hit the bow of the ship behind us. The following day we entered the port city of Kóga for water, supplies, and fuel. No shore leave was granted, and we remained restless on the ship. A few hours after docking, however, the air-raid signal was sounded, and we were ordered ashore. As we reached the sugar cane fields on the outskirts of the city, the raid started.

The raid against the port—bombing and persistent machine gunning by the Grumman F6Fs—was devastating. Most of our fleet was sunk or seriously damaged. The commander and officers of my ship had to swim and were in the water for eight hours before reaching shore. Not only was our ship lost, but all of the supplies for our unit were gone too. The soldiers who were stranded were temporarily assigned to the Taiwan Military Headquarters. Using the school building of the Kokukin National School as the base, we were well prepared for the regular air-raids at night by B-29s, plus the occasional daytime raids. At every screech of the siren, we ran for our underground bomb shelter. It was a harrowing and frustrating time, not being able to fight back at my enemy. Every day I hated the Americans more and more.

This daily hiding and escaping went on for about a month. Finally, we got the order to reboard the ship for departure. Looking at its many bullet holes, I had my doubts as to the ability of the ship to remain afloat during the remaining voyage. Fortunately our sailing was postponed, due to heavy seas and the general war situation around the Philippines. As it turned out, that was our last attempt to move into a forward area. Our unit was assigned to the 157th Airport Battalion Supply Company of the Air Force of Taiwan. There were no training planes available for our unit and so my dream of becoming a pilot remained just that, a dream.

We worked around the clock, refueling and keeping the airplanes of the special attack force in flight readiness. It was unbearable for all of us, being so close to the Zeros, the fighter planes we loved, and not being able to continue our training.

There were two airports in Heitô where we were stationed. The Americans bombed the runways every day, and it was our job to fill in the bomb craters with mud and straw. Every time I looked skyward and saw enemy planes, I regretted my position. I was a patriot, my country's enemy was my enemy. I wanted to kill Americans. In defeating our Imperial forces on the islands in the Pacific, they had brought humiliation to my country. I knew that I could kill many of my enemy before I died a glorious death for my Emperor. I hated the Americans more and more as every day went by that I was not in combat.

Our billet was twenty minutes away from the main field, in a place called Tokuwaki, so there we were able to enjoy a peaceful existence surrounded by sugarcane and endless banana fields. We found the breeze warm and refreshing after our hard labor, and I always enjoyed the stillness. At night we slept under heavy mosquito nets to prevent bites from malaria-carrying mosquitoes. I can still see the white geckos (wall lizards) climbing on the ceiling above my bunk.

According to the military records, we were a part

of the defense forces in the battle of Taiwan. From January 15 until March 15, 1945, we kept the planes supplied with fuel and ammunition around the clock. There was no time for sleep at all; not even a brief nap. We pulled guard duty along with our other work assignments. On March 26, I was given my post at the sugar refinery that produced fuel for our planes. But just before we were to report for duty, I received a dispatch ordering me to report to a secret airfield. One of my friends, a classmate, was assigned to take my place at the refinery. Normally an obedient soldier, he vigorously protested the assignment. Our commanding officer, I was later told, had to slap him before he reluctantly reported for duty. The sky was cloudy that day, heavy with rain clouds, so we were surprised by an unidentified American plane. It dropped *tsurumaki* bombs (parachute bombs) over the refinery. My replacement ran for an air-raid shelter but, before reaching it, was killed instantly when he was hit in the head by a piece of shrapnel. I have often wondered if he sensed his death beforehand and tried to prevent it by protesting the assignment. His superior regretted sending him on duty the day he died. He had a watch belonging to the dead man that he was keeping to pass on to his relatives. Every time the watch stopped, the officer was seen to look at it and heard to say "Are you still bearing a grudge against me?"

I was extremely lucky in my new assignment. We spent many comfortable days at this secret airport, far from the daily bombings at Heitô. My records show that I participated in the Tengô air operation from March 26 until June 20, 1945.

Taiwan was occupied by my country, and all natives under the age of eighteen were drafted for service. About two hundred Taiwanese of my age were assigned to the Special Engineer Security Corps. They kept the runways mowed and did heavy labor elsewhere on the field. We often spoke to them about our lives and, since we were of similar age, at times they even invited us to their homes and entertained us. I noticed that they were even more obedient than we were and very much in control of their emotions. After all, we were their conquerors and masters, yet they showed not the slightest sign of hatred they must have felt.

Every morning I watched the large formations of American B-29s fly through the sky against the background of sun-tinted clouds. Then, one day, I heard on the communication squad radio about the nuclear bombing of Hiroshima. The next day I read about it in our newspaper. My heart was filled with hatred for the Americans. Then the war was over.

The military in Taiwan wanted to continue and to fight it out, but they finally signed the armistice. We were returned to our units as prisoners-of-war. There we started to cultivate our own food, in order to be self-sufficient, and spent time clearing up debris.

The sound of firecrackers filled the air as the Taiwanese celebrated the end of the war. Colorful ornaments decorated the streets. I could see and feel the Chinese nationalism surfacing after being suppressed for so long by the Japanese rulers. Our life as prisoners was quite good, especially in comparison to my countrymen who were detained in Russia. We had plenty of food and little outcry from the public was directed our way. I thought I was living in heaven, even though we lost the war.

I remained in Taiwan as a prisoner until March 8, 1946. Finally, on that day, we left for home on an American liberty ship. Due to the usual spring bad weather, making for an extremely rough ocean, the journey to Japan took seven days. When we finally arrived I felt the earth of my dear country again, at the port of Ootake, in Hiroshima prefecture. I was almost overcome with emotion, returning home unscathed. I was given a little money and some food, and I left on a crowded military train for Hara, my home.

There is an old Japanese saying: "Even though the country may have lost the war, the mountains and the rivers remain." I arrived to find both our old home and my somewhat aged family all intact. It was March 16th—the anniversary of my father's death.

I had mixed feelings about the American food supplies given to our people. But the fact is, that they saved us from starvation. I applied for my old job at Kokusan Denki but was turned down. The people in charge did not serve in our country's war effort and told me that I betrayed the trust the company had put in me before the war. As strange as that sounds, they felt it had been my duty to continue to work for their profit rather than to fight for my country in the war against America. Consequently, I was forced to get employment as a factory worker for two years.

As the days went by and I heard the news of my classmates' deaths, I was tortured by the thought, "What was the purpose of going to war?" I had not undergone much hardship in the war, nor had I been in the midst of the killing and fighting. I had not accomplished my long-cherished dream of flying a fighter plane, even for a few hours. Nor of killing myself for the sake of my country. I could not escape from the remorse I felt; the tremendous sense of guilt for what I had and had not done. I came home whole in body but not in spirit. Little by little I got away from the dirty memories of the war and started to feel the peace around me. I contemplated what I should now do with my life.

At the end of October 1947, I applied for, and was accepted by, the Labor Standards Bureau. Since my career had always been in the technical field, I had to study the legal system and the relevant laws and ordinances.

The defeat by our enemy had brought about many radical changes in our society. Our war leaders were purged from the government (many went on trial for crimes against humanity), political prisoners were released, and epoch-making civil liberties programs were activated. The once suppressed labor movement came under the protection of the new constitution, and civil servants began to appear. Every day new challenges awaited me in my job as Supervisor, at the Mishima Standards Bureau. But in a short while, I became disenchanted with the monstrous authority of the power ministries of the government. Their job, it seemed to me, was to maintain their control with little thought to the true purpose of a public servant's role of serving the public. Eventually, I reached the conclusion that I could not work in the midst of the continuous, nasty, competition between my co-workers. I wondered long and hard about to whom the administration belongs, before I decided to leave my secure position. I was within a few short years of having earned a pension, yet I felt unable to remain true to myself in the position. Without discussing the decision with my wife and children, I resigned.

I began a new career in August of 1959, as Representative of Japanese Inns (*ryokan*). There I have now worked diligently for over thirty years. When I began, tourism was a non-essential enterprise. Most of the companies were small and treated their employees quite poorly. I decided to use the knowledge gained in my previous position to improve the relationship between employer and employee. This new challenge renewed my faith in human nature. I felt clean and refreshed in my new life. The response to my efforts has been very rewarding.

The new constitution, written after the surrender to America, included a preamble rejecting war in general, the surrender of our right to bear arms, and a tribute to world peace. I have spent my entire life contributing to worthy causes, giving my labor to the war effort, and as the war expanded, offering my life to my country. All wartime sacrifices by me and my fellow countrymen were defined as duty to the country, and we all strived to carry out our orders blindly. After the war, after the Emperor declared himself to be human rather than divine, our thoughts began to change. We began to see how the military leaders used the divinity of Emperor Hirohito to push us all into blind service, and the eventual death of the youth of our country. We believe in the reincarnation of our honored dead. But now, with the realization of the folly of the supreme sacrifice, the souls of our young soldiers have not found a resting place.

Now, with the support of America, Japan has again risen to become a major economic force in the world. The peaceful daily life we now live has produced a feeling of contentment and tranquillity in the hearts and minds of the Japanese people. It is quite obvious to us all how splendid are the days of peace without war.

Even though Japan is seen as a rich nation, I myself am far from being well off. I belong to the majority of our population, those who belong to the working class; salary men. Lately, the news of the changes taking place in Europe has been the occasion for discussion about democracy and socialism. But the distribution of wealth will remain an impossible dream. Just thinking about which society is superior is an impossibility. Even in the midst of the poverty of the years after the war, I was able to live in contentment, for I was always surrounded by caring people, and I looked at my life as a gift of peace.

I have been healthy and blessed with a faithful wife and four fine children. I have conducted my life in a fashion similar to my ancestors. I wanted my family to have an education beyond that which I had experienced. Hatsue has been a fine wife, and between us, we accomplished most of our goals. My three sons, Kiyotaka, Tadashi, and Masato, all went on to get their degrees. Then they branched out. Kiyotaka became a bacteriologist. Tadashi a geologist, and

Masato an engineer. Just last year we completed the payment of the school loans.

Our fourth child was a girl, and we named her Takako. She blossomed into a lovely young woman, graduated from the English Literature Department of a junior college, and took a position as an assistant in a private English school, Kiddy College. It was there that she met Robert Yellin, my future son.

This is the end of Taro's biography, his thoughts and experiences so beautifully expressed. It is unusual for a Japanese person to talk about themselves in such detail. Because Taro did, I have learned that our lives were and are much the same.

When we left Shimoda, Taro expressed his desire to accompany us to the airport. "We can ride on the train with you and Helene. Have a few more hours to spend together."

"I wouldn't think of it," I responded, "it is much too far to go. Besides, Mr. Osada is going to Tokyo on business, and he has offered to drive us to Narita."

"Wonderful, I will ask Takako to drive us in her car and we can see you off at the airport."

"Taro," I exclaimed, "it is a four-and-a-half-hour drive each way. You will be spending nine hours in the car, the same amount of time we will be in the plane getting to Los Angeles. Let's just say our *Sayonara* at Robert's house."

"Jerry-San, that is not the way we do things in Japan. Takako, Hatsue and I will follow you to the air-port and say good-bye there."

We left for Narita at eleven-thirty in the morning

a few days later. Mr. Osada, Helene, and I in one car, Takako and her parents followed in another. Narita Airport is only 125 miles or so from Mishima. We reached the outskirts of Tokyo in an hour on a four lane toll road. There, the roadway narrowed to a single lane in each direction and hundreds of trucks were lined up trying to enter the elevated two-lane road that surrounds the city. We didn't arrive at Narita Airport until four in the afternoon—four and a half hours to drive 125 miles.

Our plane was scheduled to leave at 5:30 P.M. We checked our luggage and had an hour left to spend with the Yamakawas before we had to leave them for our security check. We went to a coffee shop on the concourse. I had a very difficult time trying to express my feelings. I was drained from the emotional days we had in Japan and tired from sitting in traffic for so long. I could only look at Taro and Hatsue, I couldn't bring myself to say anything. Obviously, they were feeling something as well, since neither of them attempted any conversation.

After coffee, we stood at the gate entrance awkwardly. Takako and Helene began to cry, stifling their tears with handkerchiefs. Hatsue reached out to hug me around the waist, an entirely out-of-character gesture for a Japanese person, but one that expressed to me her acceptance of our family. Taro snapped to attention, raising his right hand into a salute. I did the same to him, and we turned away and left. I must say that it was extremely emotional for me. I couldn't believe this last gesture of respect from my former enemy, now my family. The years of hatred and anguish dropped away, I was relieved of the burdens of guilt for living through the war. I felt I could get on with my life and live in peace with myself.

The Yamakawas remained at the head of the stairs, waving until we were out of sight.

We were flying back on Singapore Airlines in a new 747/400. The plane had just arrived when we approached the gate area. The pilot and crew were waiting for the passengers to disembark before they boarded for the flight to L.A. I recognized the pilot, an Englishman with whom we had flown before. When I said hello, he introduced me to his co-pilot from China, and the engineer from India. "Quite an international crew," I thought. And the cabin crew had men and women from Japan, America, and Singapore.

An hour after take-off, before the meal service started, I walked the full length of the airplane and back again, several times. My fellow passengers were, it seemed from every country. Indian women wearing saris, orientals, and caucasians in each cabin.

When I sat down, Helene and I reflected on our experiences. Our minds were reeling from the events of the past few days. The first meeting of Taro and Hatsue, the wedding and the depth of the talks with Taro in Shimoda. I thought about Robert and his life so far away from us.

Midway into the flight home, I settled back, closed my eyes and began meditating. In the stillness and silence of my mind, a thought quietly surfaced. Here I am, on a space ship, locked in place for nine hours with people from all over the world. Our lives were in the hands of the engineers who designed and built our ship and the pilot who sat at the controls. Each of us had our own space, enough food. All we were meant to do was sit back and enjoy our journey, each in our own way. There was order in our surroundings, in our flight plan. Not much different from the space ship called Earth that we all lived on. What would happen, I thought, if our journey on earth was as smooth and orderly as what I was experiencing now. The thought left me as suddenly as it appeared. I opened my eyes, looked out the window at the stars in the sky, and dreamed my dreams. I had regained my innocence after carrying the memories of the war for more than forty years. I felt like a child once more. I had come home.

The letter postmarked Kanazawa, Japan arrived on March 17, Helene's birthday. It was from Kiyotaka, Taro's oldest son. It was addressed,

"Dear Parents in San Diego,"

After greetings and expressing his joy at the wedding, Kiyotaka abruptly changed the subject.

"I would like to write a line or two about my father in Numazu," he wrote. "He never spoke to his family about his experiences in the war. As you know, it was a dreadful experience, and it meant not only the loss of the war, but it also overturned all of our values. It was the end of the world. The major part of the responsibility lies with the rulers of Japan at that time. But most of the generation, including my father, kept their mouths shut and became the foundation of today's Japanese prosperity. I have criticized it at times, saying it was a passive method. But I do understand that the experience of that generation was devastating.

"It was through your wedding speech that I realized that my father was able to accept the end of the war for the first time, through the wedding of his beloved daughter, my sister, Takako."

Signed,

Kiyotaka Yamakawa

AFTERWORD

JAPAN IS LIKE home to me now. We have friends and family there, the neighborhoods are familiar. We visit Robert and Takako at least once a year. It does not seem likely that our son will ever move back to the United States. It saddens us sometimes to think of our children and grandchildren so far away, but I like what my family stands for. That is what life is all about. We are fulfilled through their happiness, their purposeful life. I am grateful for having had the opportunity to expand my family ties to include my new Japanese family.

Taro and I became grandfathers when Kentaro was born in 1989 and Simon in 1991. When we visit the grandchildren in Japan, they speak to Helene and me in English and to Taro and Hatsue in Japanese. To them, the only difference between their grandfathers is that I respond to Grandpa and he to Ojiisan. We sometimes walk on the rocky beach of Suruga Bay with our grandsons, stop and skip stones across the water, and admire the view of snow-capped Mount Fuji in the distance.

That is the legacy of the fathers.